Hussein Chalayan

Hussein Chalayan

Texts by
Judith Clark
Susannah Frankel
Pamela Golbin
Emily King
Rebecca Lowthorpe
Sarah Mower

Drawings by
Hussein Chalayan

Edited by
Robert Violette

RIZZOLI
NEW YORK

New York Paris London Milan

CONTENTS

TRANSCENDENCE

SPEED AND MOTION

METAMORPHOSIS

CONTENTS

First published in the United States of America 2011 by

Rizzoli International Publications, Inc.
300 Park Avenue South
New York, NY 10010
www.rizzoliusa.com

Edited and devised by Robert Violette
www.violetteeditions.com

Designed by Studio Frith
www.studiofrith.com

Robert Violette would like to express his very grateful thanks to
Milly Patrzalek and Claudia Bothe, of Hussein Chalayan, for their boundless
support, enthusiasm and assistance in originating this book, and especially
to Hussein Chalayan himself for this generous and unprecedented collaboration.
Additional thanks, for their commitment and invaluable work, are due
to art director Frith Kerr and Amy Preston of Studio Frith; to Tamsin Perrett,
Naomi McIntosh, Steve Evans and Kate Crockett for Violette Editions; to copyeditor
Amoreen Armetta; to Charles Miers and Ellen Nidy of Rizzoli Publications, Inc.;
and to the esteemed authors of the texts in this publication, Judith Clark, Susannah
Frankel, Pamela Golbin, Emily King, Rebecca Lowthorpe and Sarah Mower, without
whom any serious interpretation of work by Hussein Chalayan would be incomplete.

ISBN-13 978-0-8478-3386-3
Library of Congress control number 2010940538
2012 2013 2014 2015 / 10 9 8 7 6 5 4 3 2

Retouching and pre-press by Violette Editions
Printed and bound in China

Frontispiece: Hussein Chalayan having his coffee cup read by Gülsüm Metin.
Photographs by Marcus Tomlinson.
Above: Hussein Chalayan, self-portrait, old Athens airport, 2003.
Back cover: *Sakoku*, Spring/Summer 2011. Still from a video by Hussein Chalayan;
director of photography, Martin Testar.

Front cover:
Photograph by Richard Avedon
Carmen Kass and Audrey Marnay, New York, May 1998.
Originally published in *The New Yorker*, 20 July 1998.
Photograph (and pages 206–07) © The Richard Avedon Foundation.

EDITOR'S NOTE

Robert Violette

As Rebecca Lowthorpe observes later in this book, Hussein Chalayan likes to ask questions, lots of questions, of everyone and everything he contacts. This unrelentingly inquisitive disposition drives him, and propagates the fabric of ideas that underpin his work.

Such is the breadth of Chalayan's investigations, that our first conversations regarding this book included numerous additional topics ranging from Time and Religion to Serious Play and Geometry. Together we refined our selection to the essential themes presented here, which move back and forth through the years, illustrating territories staked out by Chalayan's diverse collections, films, installations and other projects.

While these themes provide a useful means of navigating the complex origins of Chalayan's creations, they are in some ways inadequately subtle as a means of demonstrating nuances. So we rely on the designer's own words, on the erudite chapter introductions by Judith Clark and on the careful annotations for each collection by Pamela Golbin. This detail is critical because, as Clark once wrote to me, 'Chalayan's references and allusions can be so internalised as to be virtually a private language, an idiom less and less explicit. In that idiosyncratic sense, Chalayan is the most stylistically a-historical of designers.'

With Chalayan's independence in mind, and from a resolutely catholic design perspective, Emily King has written a masterful study of his unique position in art and design. Susannah Frankel and Sarah Mower, who have experienced Chalayan's now legendary shows since the first, telescope in: Frankel offers a rich personal narrative of Chalayan's impact on fashion, while Mower's forceful interview probes his formative years in Cyprus. Capping this, Lowthorpe tells us how Chalayan has managed admirably to extend his work by designing collections for brands that have sustained him.

This book would be incomplete without what is, for Chalayan especially, his most telling visual contribution: hundreds of his own drawings, from a collection of thousands, from which all of his work has been and continues to be developed. Yet another demonstration of this designer's boundless virtuosity.

R I T U A L S
R E N E W E D

Emily King

A Hussein Chalayan fashion show is a highly charged event. Renowned for his mastery of catwalk drama since student days, the designer is able to generate a hum of anticipation from even the most jaded of fashion audiences. In archive video footage of Chalayan's collections dating back as far as the late 1990s, the excited response of the crowd – which includes fashion editors deep into week-long stints of watching back-to-back shows – is audible. Not just the peels of applause greeting spectacular effects, you can also hear nervous muttering and confused outbursts as viewers try to make sense of Chalayan's more ambiguous theatrical and sartorial confrontations.

These videos, which are available on Chalayan's website, are not pieces in themselves, but records of live events. As such, they give an impression both of the work and its reception. The earlier footage, in particular, takes you back to an era when fashion was a relatively inaccessible field and shows were staged for an informed coterie. With hindsight, this kind of happening seems almost quaint. Over the last few seasons, live streaming has rendered fashion shows indistinguishable from fashion advertising, transforming the catwalk from a site for theatrical happenings into a means of generating consumer information.

In February 2000 Chalayan produced one of his most spectacular fashion week coups de théâtre, his Autumn/Winter 2000 collection titled *Afterwords*. That this show took place just after the 1999 launch of the fashion website Style.com is coincidental, yet *Afterwords* does seem to represent the epitome of the thematically driven fashion ritual in the immediate pre-online age. Twenty minutes long, *Afterwords* was accompanied by a live soundtrack performed by an unaccompanied Bulgarian female choir. Its setting was a schematic living room: four chairs, a coffee table, a shelf of domestic objects and what appears to be a TV screen. The first thing the audience saw was a family – father, mother, grandmother and two daughters – sitting on chairs that were obscured by their clothing. They stood, gathered and retied the loose fabric around their legs, and exited stage left, leaving their seats to be removed by white-coated agents. The models wore a series of outfits that, in spite of their minimal appearance, were infused with detail suggesting something that might be worn by a member of the choir. Entering from a door at the back of the stage, they skirted the furniture and posed. Certain pieces, an extraordinary dress created entirely from

8

Afterwords, Autumn/Winter 2000.
Show photograph by Chris Moore.
See 'Migration' ▲ p. 240.

tightly spaced fabric florets, and a shearling coat with integral gloves, were met with spontaneous rounds of applause.

Around seven minutes in the models started removing objects from the shelves, among them an umbrella that fitted into an appropriately tailored pocket and a leather pouch that tied inside a coat. At 15 minutes four models entered the stage wearing only neutral-toned shifts, they occupied themselves with the sitting room chairs and within minutes had transformed the chair covers into dresses. The audience whooped with surprise as two of the white-coated crew folded the chair frames into suitcases. Then the finale: a fifth model appeared, removed the centre of the coffee table and stepped in. Grasping a pair of handles she drew the table up, telescope fashion, until it became an A-line skirt that hooked onto her waistband. Walking slowly, the wooden bell swaying round her calves she joined her fellows. There were shouts of approval, rapturous applause, the choir reached a climax and the lights dimmed.

According to certain criteria, *Afterwords* conforms absolutely to the conventions of a fashion show. Between a quarter and half an hour long and displaying roughly one outfit every 30 seconds, its span and rate were probably that of the bulk of the collections that season. Yet, in other ways, *Afterwords* is much closer to a piece of theatre. It followed a narrative path, albeit an indirect one, and played on expectation, in particular employing suspense to brilliant effect. Comparing it with the shows created by Chalayan's late contemporary Alexander McQueen, also a master of runway spectacle, *Afterwords* is striking for its concentration on human scale. McQueen's collection for Autumn/Winter 2000 was a tribal-apocalyptic fusion titled *Eshu*. Showing in an enormous industrial space, he had the models stalk down a shale-strewn catwalk with aggressive strides. At the risk of over simplifying: where McQueen inspired awe in his audience, Chalayan gently tips their balance, creating wonder through incongruity.

The theme of *Afterwords* is the plight of the refugee. Thinking in particular about members of his own family, Turkish Cypriots who were forced to leave their homes in Cyprus in the 1960s before the pro-Greek coup in 1974, Chalayan imagined scenarios in which people are required to flee carrying what they are able. At the start of the piece the set connotes the informal yet ritualised aspects of family life: drawing-room entertaining and communal television watching. Considering the possibility of sudden exile, Chalayan suggested the possibility of new rituals, ones of dismantling and displacement.

By creating a ceremony out of necessity, the fugitive generates a sense of control. Just as the Old Testament makes sense of exile in stories and verse, *Afterwords* suggests you might be able to enact and mitigate its impact using objects and dress.

The narrative content of this and other Chalayan collections raises questions about the relationship between what something is and what it represents. A fashion show is in itself a highly ritualised affair, a consumerist harvest festival promising the possibility of constant renewal. By bringing elements such as the family onto the catwalk, a grouping that raises the spectre of ageing and death, Chalayan creates a powerful friction against the idea of a seasonal collection. Chalayan's designs are often called conceptual, a term that seems to imply fashion itself, fashion pure and simple, is a no-concept quantity. This is hugely misleading. Fashion is an enormous idea, a vast and complex fiction in which many of us play a willing part. It is the extraordinary premises of fashion as a whole that makes it the perfect vehicle for counter-narratives and conflicting ideas.

One particularly contradictory aspect of fashion is the expectation of surprise. That is, surprise comes as no surprise. Superlatives are normalised. *Fabulous!*, *amazing!* and *fantastic!* denote nothing more than run of the mill. Within this framework, Chalayan is still able to provoke genuine astonishment often by eschewing the spectacular. There are no fireworks in *Afterwords*. Although dressing yourself in your furniture is an extraordinary thing to do, the models executed their moves in a strikingly awkward, everyday fashion. Their arms strained over their backs to pull zips, and their mouths pursed in concentration as they buttoned and tied straps and flaps. The process is ordinary yet compelling and created a focus on the meaning embodied in mundane physical gestures that brought the performance close to certain strands of contemporary dance. Considering the apparent centrality of the human form in fashion as a whole, it is extraordinary how unexceptional movements can become radical runway gestures. The discipline's rigid codes can be challenged by the smallest tugs at its fabric.

Among the most severe of fashion's rules is its twice-yearly demand for novelty. Most designers, Chalayan included, find this rhythm particularly brutal and it can appear that they play out their battle with the clock at the runway shows, requiring that their audiences spend longer waiting than watching. Beyond the purgatory of this delay, time in every sense and at every scale is at the heart of the fashion ritual, from the hours it takes to sew a couture dress to the telescoping cycles of revival. As mentioned previously, the dawn of instant access to information has added a whole new dimension to fashion's engagement with the moment. Runway minutes have collapsed into advertising intervals, and some fashion brands now offer the chance to purchase a look the instant it appears on the catwalk. In an interview published in 1994 Chalayan said of fashion, 'I am not against it or for it, I accept it as a condition.' This is a position that he still holds, yet what *it* is, the nature of the fashion ritual, has changed enormously since then.

Ever cognisant of this situation, among the consistent features of the rituals that Chalayan has created for the catwalk over the last 10 years is an engagement with technology. He showed a mechanically animated dress in February 1999 as the finale of the Autumn/Winter 1999 collection *Echoform*. Suggestive of aeroplane construction, it consists of two fibreglass and resin panels fastened with metal clips. Just as the forms of aircraft invoke certain fetishistic feelings, so the dress conforms to an idealised feminine shape, creating a sense of breasts, waist and hips

Echoform, Autumn/Winter 1999.
Show photograph by Chris Moore.
Model: Audrey Marnay.
See 'Speed and Motion' 🎩 p. 90.

independent of the form underneath. On the catwalk, the dress was worn by a model with a winningly impish expression. She stood quite still, amusement playing on her lips, as a series of flaps moved around the neck and hem and a large central panel shifted to reveal her bare stomach. The routine was akin to the series of preparations before a flight, the movements of the air stewards gesturing to the emergency exits echoing those of the aircraft's wing flaps flexing in anticipation. From the point of view of the passenger, this dance signals the abnegation of control and the submission to the machine.

Since 1999, Chalayan has returned to the theme of human passivity in the face of technology several times, among the most recent outings being his Spring/Summer 2007 collection titled *One Hundred and Eleven*. Addressing the evolution of fashion over the last 111 years, it featured a set of six remotely controlled dresses that morphed from one style to another in a series of elegant mechanical movements. Two thirds of the way through the 15-minute show, a model took centre stage and stood stock still while her long, late-Victorian style skirt rose to her knees. This routine was repeated five times with Edwardian becoming flapper, 1950s New Look evolving into 1960s modern and so on. The animation of the materials was clipped yet ceremonial, making the process appear like a robotic investiture. For the finale, a model arrived on stage wearing a broad-brimmed hat and a sheer outfit. Over the course of about 20 seconds she was mechanically undressed, left naked but for her headgear. Nudity on the catwalk has long-since ceased to be shocking, yet, for all the uninhibited claps and cheers from the audience, this image of cyborg stripping remains distinctly disturbing.

In the introduction to a collection of essays titled *The Invention of Tradition* the historian Eric Hobsbawm allied the idea of tradition to 'ritualised practices' and argued that traditions differed from 'routines' or 'conventions' in terms of their 'symbolic function.'[1] The thesis of the book

[1] Eric Hobsbawm and Terence Ranger, eds., *The Invention of Tradition* (Cambridge: Cambridge University Press, 1983).

One Hundred and Eleven, Spring/Summer 2007.
Show photographs by Chris Moore.
See 'Metamorphosis' ○ p. 132.

as a whole is that new traditions and their accompanying rituals are invented 'when a rapid transformation of society weakens or destroys the social patterns for which "old" traditions had been designed.' In his own chapter Hobsbawm concentrates on Europe in the late 19th and early 20th centuries, a period when various mechanisms prompted profound and far-reaching social and political change. Among the invented rituals of this period was that of mass sport, an expression, according to Hobsbawm of 'the workers' consciousness of their existence as a separate class.'

With this in mind, it is interesting to consider the recent flourish of new rituals. Mass sport, in particular football, keeps going strong, but, no longer an expression of working class identity (an identity that, arguably, bit the dust during Margaret Thatcher's prime ministership), it now belongs to tribes that are defined by their consumer habits. You no longer have to belong, you simply have to buy, a situation that allows support for Chelsea Football Club to be as fervent in Osaka as in London SW10. In parallel with the rise of sport as a cross-class, pan-cultural phenomenon of ritualised tribal and seasonal consumption, fashion has also come to occupy a place in broader social and economic circles than ever before. To an extent, and in spite of the obvious truth that men and women move between fields, sport and fashion are the masculine and feminine expressions of the same impulse.

In recent years fashion shows, like the football matches, have reached a mass spectatorship through the Internet and extensive press coverage. Developing the notion of the collections as a contemporary harvest festival, the runway show enacts the possibility of an eternal present, dressing up the relentless push to consume in the guise of new beginnings. On a macabre note, it disguises the march toward death as a parade of unflagging novelty. Discussing the subject, Chalayan asks, 'Where else but the front row would you find such a group of people: a movie star, a singer, a politician and a banker's wife?' The obvious answer to this question is, of course, at a football match (who can forget Bill Clinton chatting in the stands with Mick Jagger in South Africa in 2010?). In the case of both fashion and football, the celebrities are less there to watch than be seen watching. Their presence is mutual confirmation of their own power and that of the fashion house or sporting body, joined in the affluent defiance of the progress of time.

The birth of tradition and the invention of ritual are common subjects in the art of the last 40 years. Responding in part to the dramatic social change that has taken place since the 1960s, artists have used film and performance to raise questions about coded behaviour. Of works by recent generations, the films of Matthew Barney stand out for their intricate and extended ritualistic activities, involving fantastical creatures in elaborate fictional settings. At the other end of the spectrum, Jeremy Deller explores existing local or niche ceremonies, often raising questions about their purpose and meaning by displacing them from one location or medium to another. At the 2009 Manchester Festival, for example, he enlisted a disparate set of concerns including a Hindu bagpiping band, a recreation of Britain's oldest tearoom and a troop of mobile libraries into a new kind of civic procession. Many of the rituals that Deller explores are of recent invention and, in creating new settings for these rituals, he is adding a further layer to what are themselves relatively fresh ceremonies. Effectively he is reinventing invented ritual – rebirthing tradition, perhaps.

Deller's and Barney's work is shown in art contexts: commercial gallery shows, museum exhibitions, biennales and so on. As with fashion, these various settings are subject to a level of expectation and a degree of ritualistic behaviour and, just as with a fashion show, while an art

performance or film might be about ritual, at the same time it is a kind of ritual in itself. Questions about what something is and what it is about apply equally across fields. Over the last decade Chalayan has worked between disciplines, making films and pieces intended to be shown in galleries or festivals as well as more tightly defined fashion works. Significantly his art films are listed on his website, but are not accessible online. Sold to private collectors or institutions, works such as the *Anaesthetics* (2004), *Compassion Fatigue* (2006) or *I Am Sad Leyla (Üzgünüm Leyla)* (2010) are treated as collectible products rather than information.

Looking at the earliest of these, at just over 20 minutes long, *Anaesthetics* is not only the length of a fashion show, it also shares certain aspects with Chalayan's work for the catwalk. There are the white-coated agents playing an ambiguous servant/master role, there are the props – a rotating stage furnished with a multipurpose wooden structure – and there are the clothes. Yet the film does not contain nearly enough looks to make a collection, and, in terms of non-sartorial content, it is a great deal more dense and detailed than any fashion format would allow. Broken into 11 short chapters, the overriding theme is the role of formalised behaviour and technology in numbing us to the pain of living. The first episode is a wigging ceremony involving a geisha-style headdress that leaves a woman's face

A cotton and silk chiffon dress and geisha veil worn in the film *Anaesthetics*, 2004, by Hussein Chalayan, as exhibited in *B-Side* at Spring Projects, London, 2010. Photographs by Noah Da Costa, courtesy Spring Projects.

Anaesthetics, 2004.
Stills from a film by Hussein Chalayan,
featuring Bennu Gerede.

hidden by a veil, her vision obscured. After ripping off the hairpiece in a swift, angry gesture, the female lead plays a central role in most of what follows. Chalayan's point appears to be that ritual oppresses everyone, but it oppresses women most of all.

The film touches on a range of issues – nourishment, birth, childhood, sex, religion, family life, violence as entertainment and cultural conflict. Uniting these issues is the simultaneous enactment and repression through ritual. In one of the film's key scenes the woman appears to regurgitate the body of Christ while a man dressed in a dog collar looks on approvingly. In spite of her submissive kneeling position and demure dress, she confronts the viewer with something quite revolting. It is hard to watch, yet the character seems to find relief in self-disgust. The piece ends with an episode set within the family. Our heroine is seated on a chair by the white-coated functionaries, her chin resting on a prop and her face inspected by cameras that are embedded in the furniture. After being photographed in the style of a scientific specimen – full face, left profile, right profile – she is rotated for the entertainment of her parents, her husband and her child. Although they look pleased and even laugh, her expression remains stony.

In bringing up these kinds of relationships, Chalayan raises significant questions about the autobiographical content of his work. We all have a family of sorts and when we see one in art the leap from reading the work to life is automatic. Thinking along similar lines, it is possible to interpret all Chalayan's themes, from the family and migration through science and technology, in the most personal of ways. Coming from a Turkish Cypriot background, but having been educated and working in London, Chalayan is keenly aware of the ritualised elements of the behaviour around him. His work springs from personal observation on every level, and he often puts us in something like his position, that of a curious outsider looking on at an apparently well-established yet somewhat obscure ceremony.

In his recent work *I Am Sad Leyla (Üzgünüm Leyla)*, shown at Lisson Gallery in 2010, Chalayan transposed a piece of Turkish musical culture to a London art setting. Breaking down a filmed version of a classical song into four elements, he placed the voice, the singer (represented by a life-sized sculpture that acted as a screen for a projection of the singer's face), the orchestra and the performance in separate galleries. As well as being an inverse metaphor for the piecemeal way that this music has evolved over time, the dismantlement also allowed art viewers to walk their usual course, moving from gallery to gallery at their own pace. A millefeuille of musical and art ritual, the piece was, above all, a compelling argument for the beauty of the song.

Chalayan's unwillingness to submit entirely to the codes of fashion coupled with his unusual position vis-à-vis art have led to his being at one step remove not only from the rituals that he documents, but also from the conventions of the worlds that he inhabits and operates within. It's an approach that gives him enormous creative freedom, yet in many ways is problematic. In spite of his thematic consistency, nothing in his work can be assumed; everything has to be thought afresh. More than challenging the

I Am Sad Leyla (Üzgünüm Leyla), 2010.
Installation by Hussein Chalayan,
Lisson Gallery, London, 2010.
Photograph courtesy Lisson Gallery.

designer, it also tests the audience, depriving them of the standard disciplinary frameworks in which to interpret what they see. Chalayan has described his aim as 'creating a bridge between different worlds and disciplines.' One way to view his present interdisciplinary, indeterminate situation is that he has made this bridge and now he's standing on it. While not engendering much in terms of comfort and ease, his position has the merit of a vantage point that is quite unique.

BORDER
CROSSING

Susannah Frankel

It is October 2010 and, in a modest, white-walled art gallery in the heart of the Marais district of Paris, the fashion designer Hussein Chalayan is showing his Spring/Summer 2011 collection. Far from the madding crowd, and seemingly a million miles away from the brouhaha that the twice-yearly international womenswear collections normally entail, Chalayan's offering takes the form of a short film. A single, spotlit model mimics the choreography of the traditional runway presentation but there's no throbbing soundtrack, attention-seeking styling and hair and make-up or over-crowded seating plan. An audience that can be counted on 10 fingers takes the place of the usual circus. Chalayan – dressed, as is usual, in unassuming black jeans and sweater – is in attendance, taking the time to talk press and buyers through the proceedings, explaining both the concepts behind the collection and the construction of the garments. Both receive equal attention, now as always. Chalayan has long claimed that the primary use of narrative in his work functions to ensure that his own interest is sustained and that the clothes speak for themselves. It has tended to be the ideas and stories surrounding his collections that have driven Chalayan. These are also the elements that have captivated anyone with more than a passing interest in the history of fashion, as Chalayan's tales have added considerable depth to his designs. In the gallery, on rails at either side of the screen hangs his collection in the flesh, enabling visitors to touch and look at the clothes up close. There's an apparently simple lightweight black wool dress here, a sweet godet skirt in white cotton viole there. Colour blocking, in this designer's hands, is as subtle as it is unexpected: dove grey with burnt orange and beige, for example. The ubiquitous summer floral comes with its own shadow adding a discreet sense of melancholy to its effect.

The collection is called *Sakoku* – literally translated as 'locked country'. The title refers to the name of Japan's foreign relations policy from 1639 to 1868 dictating that, with very few exceptions, no foreigner could enter and no native could leave on penalty of death. Exploring what Chalayan states are the more surreal aspects of Japanese culture, *Sakoku* focused, above all, on disembodiment, a subject to which he has returned again and again. Chalayan writes of this interest in his notes to the film: 'Japan is saturated with disembodied experiences in a decentred space where event is born out of the choreography of ceremony and the simulation of thought.'

Sakoku, Spring/Summer 2011.
Still from a video by Hussein Chalayan.
See 'New Anthropology' ☂ p. 224.

Three months before *Sakoku* premieres, and Chalayan is ensconced in his central London studio. On a laptop is what he calls his 'concept file': a collection of words and images gathered on a recent trip to Japan, originally pulled together simply because he liked them or they piqued his interest in some way. This will soon, painstakingly, be worked into a more unified form. It might only be expected that when a designer such as Chalayan chooses to base his collection on a specific place – a country where he is a tourist (the role of tourist being another of his enduring fascinations) – the end result would be less than literal. Chalayan has thought about water, he tells me, and the fact that Japan is an island somehow longing to return to the depths. An image of a tree, the branches of which are heavy with cherry blossoms and which is threatened by a looming tsunami, appears on his laptop screen. This reference will become part of *Sakoku*, as waves of silk draping across the surface of a structured bodice. In an earthquake prone country, every moment is monumental, the designer reasons. Another photograph is on Chalayan's screen: shot from above, a group of male, Japanese executives sit at a matt black boardroom table while the walls fall in around them. This idea will find its way into the clothing as 'collapsing' panels, Chalayan says. The aforementioned floral print has its roots in a snapshot of a row of single flowers. Flower arranging is an integral part of Japanese culture, the designer explains, here is the antithesis of a bouquet.

In a separate file labelled 'design' Chalayan's own drawings are gathered. For each collection there are literally hundreds of these, from rough sketches – made, for example, while at a kabuki performance – to drawings of finished garments. Increasingly detailed patterns and fabric descriptions show the way in which, slowly but surely, most of Chalayan's thoughts are translated into garments. Specifically, in *Sakoku*, Chalayan explores the prevalence of shadow references in Japanese culture – manifest, for example, in shadow theatre – and found in the designer's collection in his choice of print and fabric, such as the use of opaque fabric juxtaposed with panels of iridescent mesh. Then there's *Haiku*, a section in which bonded, chiffon dresses are draped individually to form the word *sonzaisuru*, meaning 'to exist', although only a Japanese speaker would ever be able to decipher it.

Sakoku, then, was an immaculately executed and carefully thought out affair. And if the end result, as far as presentation is concerned, was very different from the blockbuster shows with which Chalayan, in London in the mid-1990s, made his name, its creation involved the sum of similar parts nonetheless. Characterising Chalayan's work since he started out has been a preoccupation with symbolising ideas through the structural and design elements of clothing, and a fascination with and commitment to technological advancement and innovative, highly complex proportion and cut, as well as the process of editing his original ideas. Only those wishing to unravel the end result will ever be fully aware of the thought process behind his finished collections.

'I work like a [film] director, I think,' he tells me, 'framing things that already exist. But if you go and have dinner at someone's house and you enjoy it, you don't have to know all the ingredients, do you?'

It is, in fact, an approach more familiar to the artist than the fashion designer. And if it seems somewhat cerebral, especially seen in the context of the largely ephemeral and more obviously commercially driven fashion arena, equally significant is Chalayan's warmly expressed fascination with humanity – anthropologically, socially and culturally – that invests his whole oeuvre with an emotional strength that is as precious as it is rare. Whichever way one chooses to look at it, Chalayan is not in the business of crafting, say, the perfect black cashmere sweater or pair of black trousers – although he has proved in the past that he can do this also. Instead, the value of his own-label designs lies in their difference. In today's over-saturated market, Chalayan's voice rings out, if not loudly, then certainly with a clarity that makes it instantly recognisable to those already familiar with his language, not to mention highly appealing to any newcomer looking for something that ensures they stand out in a crowd.

Much has been written about the value of biography to criticism. There are those who argue that any life story is irrelevant and that a more purist approach pays attention to creative output alone. Others find a more personal reading to be revealing – the understanding of the psychological and cultural makeup of any creator adds to understanding of their work. In the case of Chalayan, whose work has often been infused with his own history, it seems nothing short of obstructive to separate the two. Most often mentioned is that Chalayan is a Turkish Cypriot. Any correlation may be quite literal. For example, look closely at the seemingly Hawaiian-style prints that characterise the designer's Spring/Summer 2004 collection, *Temporal Meditations*, and these prints turn out to depict the Turkish Cypriot seafront complete with the requisite high-rise architecture that any beach holiday resort today has succumbed to. In the print's background, images of historical battle scenes between the Ottomans and Venetians hint at less picturesque truths about the continuously war-torn island. Less obvious is the fact that, while working on this collection, Chalayan also actually collaborated with a genetic anthropologist who performed a DNA test on him and helped him trace not only his own genetic makeup but also that of the different ethnic groups that inhabit island. From his mother (mitochondrial DNA), Chalayan was told he inherited the first fully sequenced human mitochondrial DNA, the Cambridge Reference Sequence which is common in Europe. His Y chromosome (male line) is Viking.

Detail of print designed by Hussein Chalayan for *Temporal Meditations*, Spring/Summer 2004.

'Knowing about the DNA sequences I've inherited from my parents did not suddenly mean that I would start to identify myself with Continental Europe, with Swedes, Danes, or the English, or to deny my Turkishness,' Chalayan wrote in *anOther Magazine* in 2007. 'But it really made me wonder about who we think we are, and whether our connections to geography and our definitions of identity are as set as we think they are.'

More often, autobiographical contact is less specific. Chalayan's obsession with flight and migration, say, is presumably rooted at least in part in his being required to travel from place to place by air as a child just as he does to visit his relatives – or vice versa – to this day. With this in mind, some of his earliest work was crafted in Tyvek, printed with the words *par avion*,

and could be folded up into an envelope and sent through the post. Also suggestive of a nomadic lifestyle was Chalayan's Autumn/Winter 1998 collection, *Panoramic*, in which knitted jackets were protectively cocoon shaped and came with their own knitting needles attached. For this designer's highly inquisitive mind, any interest soon reaches beyond personal experience, however. Air travel is a continuing fascination for Chalayan – he also directed a short film on the subject titled *Anaesthetics* (2004), explaining that, for him, it represents one of the many ways in which violence is hidden through codes of behaviour. Cleverly designed seating, in-flight refreshment, entertainment and artificial air, Chalayan believes, lull travellers into a false sense of security, as if they've never left the ground.

'I don't really feel at home anywhere,' he says. 'In Cyprus, which is really my family hub, I feel like an alien. I don't go there very often any more. I go to Istanbul a lot, which I find to be an incredible magical city. I speak the language, of course. Essentially, I suppose, I think of myself as a Londoner more than anything. I'm not English, I'm a Londoner and I see London as a state in itself. I'm very interested in that as subject matter.'

Hussein Chalayan is a Turkish Cypriot born in Nicosia in 1970 but, following the divorce of his parents, moved between two entirely different cultures throughout his childhood. When living with his mother, he was immersed in his troubled and essentially insular birthplace, an environment both ravaged by infighting and steeped in mystery – as a boy Chalayan could only imagine what was happening on the Greek side of the border, forcibly established in 1974. And imagine it he did, creating superstitious codes – if he folded his pyjamas a certain way, for example – in the hope that it would ensure that his homeland would remain at peace.

'I am essentially a curious person,' he says, 'and I come from a culture which has seen two wars, from an amorphous culture, with a real history behind it. I think in a country where there is less history, less difficulty, maybe people become less prone to questioning things.'

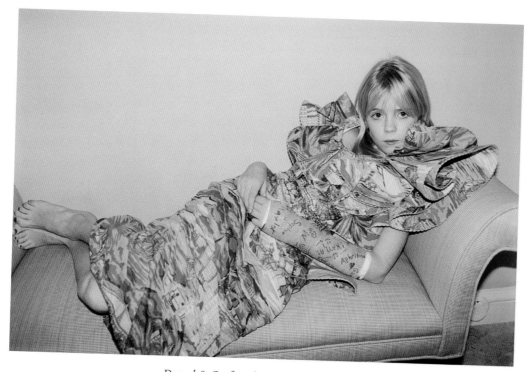

Dazed & Confused magazine, March 2004.
Photograph by Sofia Coppola. Model: Grace.

In London, with his father, Chalayan experienced a multi-cultural London, a city heaving with cosmopolitan, metropolitan life. He describes his existence in Cyprus as isolated, and very much reliant on creating an interesting world for himself. The London of Chalayan's youth, meanwhile, was exciting, over-crowded and driven by consumerism. It provided material for anyone interested (and Chalayan has always been interested) to process at leisure.

'I think that, when I was a child, and because I was an only child who came from an isolated place, I was bored all the time,' Chalayan says. 'I was alone, so I created my own world, a more colourful world. I drew a lot and created an imaginative world. That became my way of evolving, in a way. I think people in that sort of situation use their work as a means to find happiness because it's something they can always rely on, always engage with. I would travel backwards and forwards between London and Cyprus which was painful, because it meant separation, but it also allowed discovery. Even today, spending time on my own is very important to my creativity. I'm not an introvert. I'm very sociable. But there are these two polar things going on. There's definitely that duality. If you're an observant person and you're creative, the two go hand in hand, I think. You become a detached observer of things, of behaviour, or situations, of culture, of clothes...'

At boarding school in England, aged 12, Chalayan felt his position as an outsider acutely. Despite the fact that he was pale-skinned, his name was remarkable and conspicuously foreign. In fact, he saw these differences as an advantage. From an early age he was aware of an

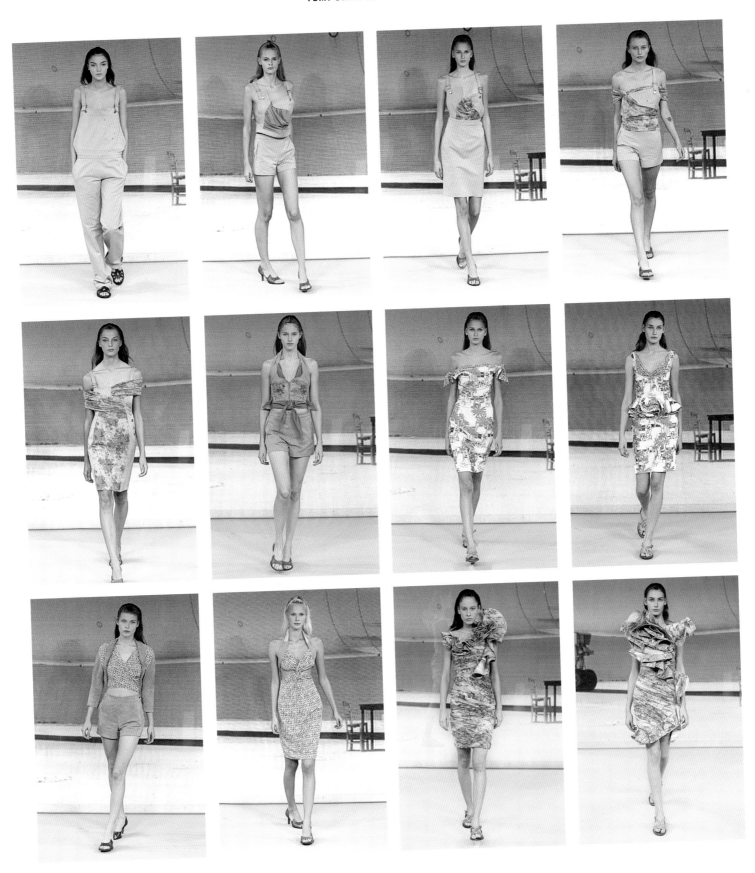

Temporal Meditations, Spring/Summer 2004.
Show photographs by Chris Moore.

Vogue magazine (US), 2004.
Photograph by Mert Alas and Marcus Piggott.
Model: Natalia Vodianova.

'otherness', as he describes it, and while many young people struggle to fit in, Chalayan was, not insignificantly, perfectly happy with that. He is drawn, he says, to those who share a similar quality to this day, unpicking the ancestry of soon-to-become friends just as he has his own.

Although, following a foundation course at college in the provincial town of Leamington Spa, Chalayan was encouraged to study fine art – specifically sculpture – he ended up enrolling for the celebrated fashion course at Central Saint Martins in London instead. This decision was driven, he has since often explained, by an interest in human beings and in women in particular. Home life in Cyprus was predominantly matriarchal and from as far back as he can remember Chalayan sketched women in situations that he found inspiring and wearing clothes to match.

'I am very excited by body image,' he says. 'There are so many things you can say about the body. I always drew women, in certain kinds of clothes, in certain kinds of environments – even when I was very young. I grew up around women in Cyprus and I liked the idea of empowering women. I was interested in the idea of a powerful woman.'

The St Martins of the period in question was a very different beast to the one it is today. Now occupying its own space, the fashion school has little contact with the arts more broadly. In Chalayan's time, and when still located in the heart of then rather brilliantly seedy Soho, this department was an integral part of a thriving art college. There were only 13 people in his year and Chalayan and his fashion contemporaries mixed freely across disciplines, benefiting as much from the neighbourhood as they did the coursework. They often worked together and visited each other's studios, feeding off one another's ideas. All the stories are true: yes, they did hide under cutting tables to avoid over-zealous security guards attempting to close up for the night, and Chalayan himself is more than happy to admit that he belonged to an impenetrable clique of people who believed entirely in their own ability and revelled in the privilege of having made it through

Hussein Chalayan, Central Saint Martins School of Art, London, c.1991.

the college's hallowed portals in the first place. Perhaps more importantly, Chalayan attributes his cross-disciplinary approach, at least partly, to this environment and remains frustrated that fashion, almost 20 years later, is seen as a poor relation to art, one that only rarely benefits from any critical discourse. In England, and for the past five years or so more than ever, a mistrust prevails of clothing that may be described as conceptual – and even of fashion per se, which is judged by many as frivolous, over-priced and pandering to the unintelligent and vain.

'There could be more critical thinking not only about fashion but design as a whole,' Chalayan says. 'Why not? It's constructive to be in your place on a critical path or discourse. You are protected in that place. If something is a good idea then why not look at it. Fashion, because it's industrial, is perceived as not having the same value as art but you can argue that art is now industrial, as well. It's part of a money market, certainly, so I don't really see what the difference is any more. If you are doing a dress that is informed by good ideas or is an amazing thing then it's as much a piece of art as somebody's painting or somebody's installation, I think.'

The fact that Chalayan has consistently argued that fashion – and design more broadly – merits a critical approach is to his credit. And he does so from a position of strength. As early as his 1993 degree collection, *The Tangent Flows*, he was challenging any preconceived notion of what clothing may be. He famously buried this, along with iron filings in a friend's back garden to see how it would decompose. Only a few seasons later, Chalayan and, of course, his most famous contemporary, Alexander McQueen, had established themselves at the forefront of not only the London fashion but also art scene. Brit Art was in the ascendant, *Sensation* was soon to open at the Royal Academy, and Chalayan and McQueen were staging the most extraordinary, grand-scale fashion experiences the world had ever seen, performances that made the traditional runway presentation appear nothing short of banal by comparison. This was not simply fashion referencing art. A mindset that decreed that the fashion show should be a cultural experience was fundamental to their way of working. Although their respective design sensibilities were very different, there was and still is a certain lightness and purity to Chalayan's aesthetic while McQueen's was more sexualised and fierce; the way they both chose to show demonstrated a need to provoke a reaction that went beyond any clothes. For Chalayan's part, everything – from the set mirrored screens for *Panoramic* (Autumn/Winter 1998), a backdrop scarred with light-up flight paths (*Ventriloquy*, Spring/Summer 2001) to the choreography, a line-up of models wearing identical chadors that diminished in size leaving

Student work by Hussein Chalayan, Mid-Warwickshire College, 1989. Photograph by Hussein Chalayan. Model: Laura Buadas Rotger.

the final woman naked (*Between*, Spring/Summer 1998) and the soundtrack, a live Bulgarian choir (*Afterwords*, Autumn/Winter 2000) – challenged fashion's parameters. And so too did the designs themselves which included egg-shaped wooden capsules worn as head coverings (*Between*), the iconic fibreglass aeroplane dress (*Echoform*, Autumn/Winter 1999) and a polished table worn as a skirt (*Afterwords*).

'When Lee [Alexander McQueen] and myself were designing in the mid-1990s there was space for it,' Chalayan says. 'There had been a recession before that. A lot of designers – Galliano, Westwood – had gone to Paris and so London was empty. Plus there was poverty so we had to find other ways of being creative and to make an impact. It was a good moment to create a new energy, a moment when there was room for newness. I think that the way we showed was new. Nothing like that had ever happened before. All the ingredients came together and that was why we were able to do what we were doing and there was such excitement around it.'

If, throughout this period, such blockbuster aspirations might have detracted from the power of the clothes, it is a measure of the aesthetic value of Chalayan's designs that this was not the case. Instead, a highly distinctive vocabulary gradually emerged. A discreet patchwork of panelling, a complex web of seams, the morphing of one garment, fabric or print into another, organic shapes cut into layers of fabric to reveal something different lurking beneath, asymmetry and clothing sprouting everything from fins and ribbons of chiffon to plain string are just some of Chalayan's signatures. His tailoring is narrow and principally boyish as opposed to more obviously masculine. His white shirts tend to be designed to be worn buttoned up to the throat. Print is generally narrative – though it might be beautiful in its own right, it has a meaning beyond that. More broadly, there is a play between the high-tech and the organic, the polished and the raw. Chalayan's clothing also tends to envelop the body, forming a protective layer and holding the wearer, as opposed to exposing her. A subtle and studied elegance is the overall effect.

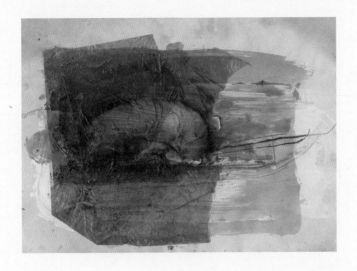

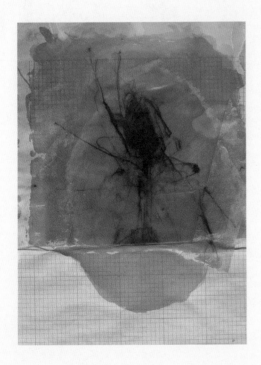

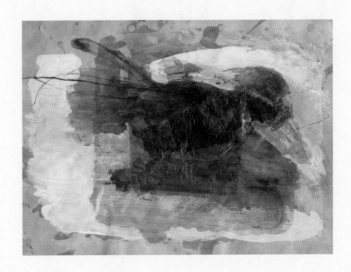

Student work, 1992.

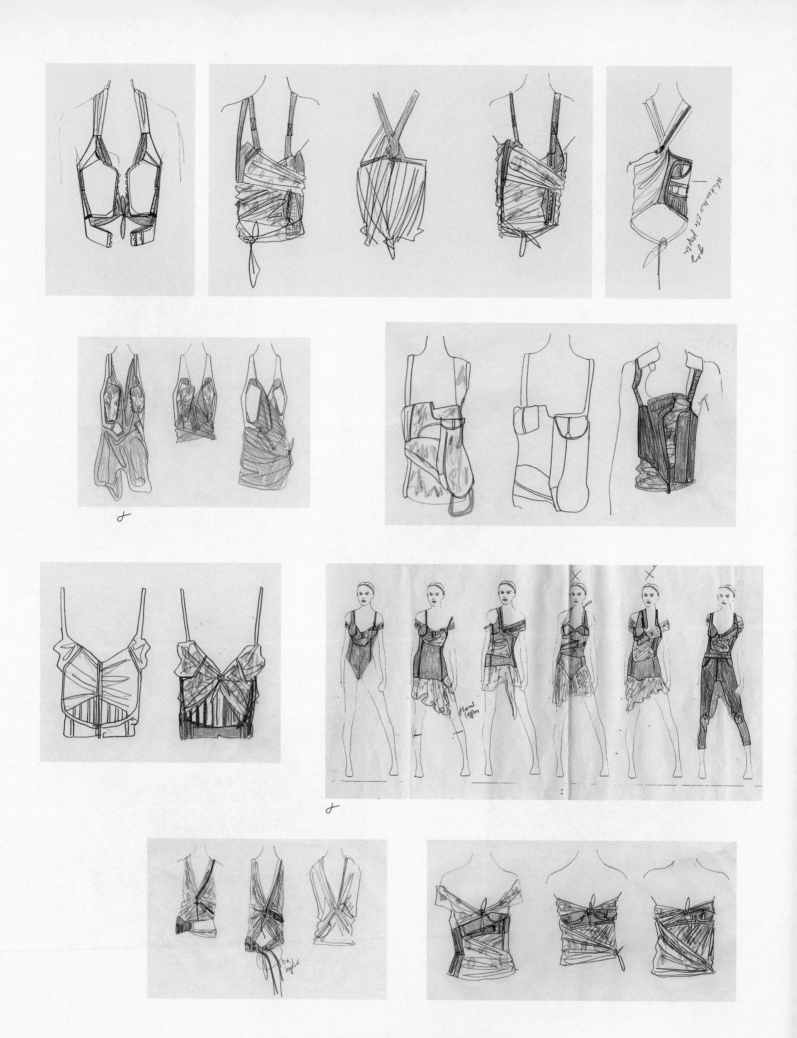

Temporal Meditations, Spring/Summer 2004.

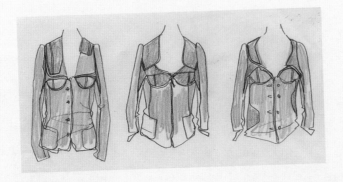
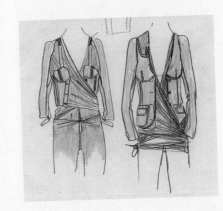

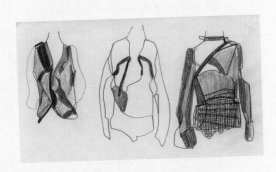
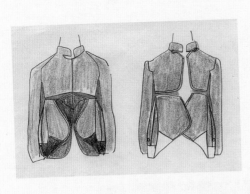
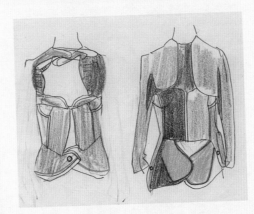

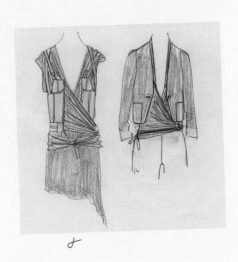

Temporal Meditations, Spring/Summer 2004.

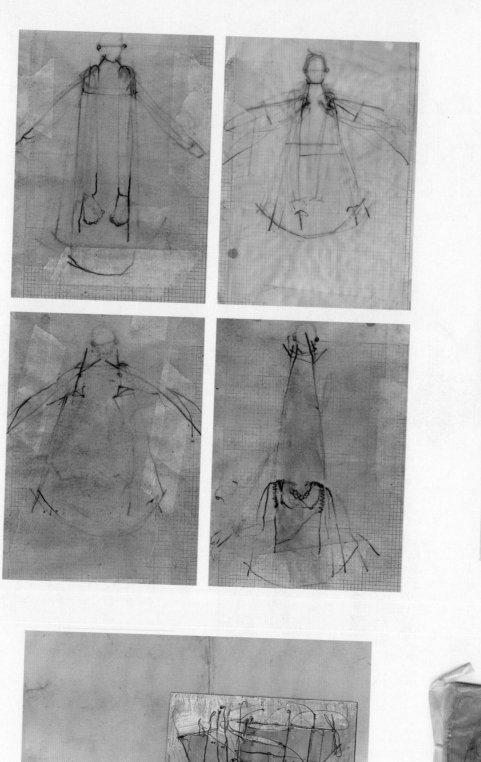
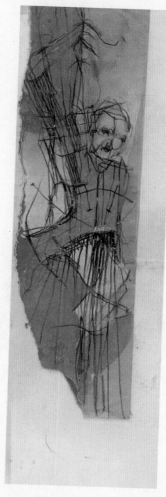
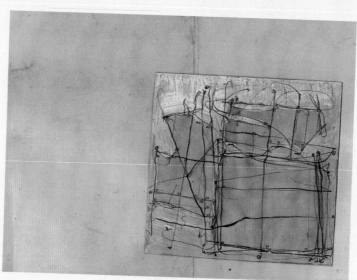

Student work, 1992.

Student work by Hussein Chalayan: Mid-Warwickshire College,
1989 (left) and Central Saint Martins, London, 1992 (right).
Photographs by Hussein Chalayan.
Models: Sharon Farreley, Özlem Özel.

Perhaps the most prevalent fashion story of the latter part of the
1990s through the first decade of the new millennium was that of the
young, independent designer employed to breathe new life into an
ageing luxury goods brand. Chalayan was appointed creative director
of TSE Cashmere in New York in 1998, which taught him about luxury,
he has said. In 2000 he developed a line of high-end clothing for
Asprey. Since 2008, the designer has found himself in the rare position
of running his own label independently. His position as artistic director
of a fashion-led collection of sportswear for Puma (owned by Pinault–
Printemps–Redoute) goes some way towards supporting Chalayan's
own-name label. With no advertising budget, and often still struggling
to make ends meet, the designer has consistently discovered new
ways to inject finance into his company thereby ensuring that his ideas
are communicated. Remarkably this includes selling limited edition
film, installations and objects to collectors of fine art the world over.
In 2010 alone Chalayan had solo exhibitions both at Lisson Gallery
and Spring Studios in London and his 2009 Design Museum show is
still travelling, most recently finding its way to Istanbul. In this, his
position is unprecedented.

Chalayan's way of showing his clothes, too, has changed. From
Medea (Spring/Summer 2002) onwards, having outgrown the relatively
parochial confines of the London collections, he moved his twice-
yearly womenswear collections to Paris, following in the footsteps of
generations of British-educated designers. The change of scenery –
and the fact that this still relatively young talent was now facing a
far larger and more seriously competitive environment – led to more

Polaroid photographs from the shoot for *Frame*, 1999 (see p. 92).
Top row: Jane How, Barbara Fourneau, John Pfeiffer.
Second row: Simon Thorogood, Audrey Marnay, Hussein Chalayan.
Third row: Eugene Soulemain, Alex de Betak, Sevim Erdal.
Bottom row: Sevil Özel, Suzanne Lee, Tomur Akpinar.

straightforward presentation that focused more intently on the clothes. Just as he proved himself to be an innovator from the moment he graduated, however, Chalayan has continued to push at the boundaries. He was among the first fashion designers to produce films as an alternative to a live runway show. Before *Sakoku* (Spring/Summer 2011), there was *Temporal Meditations* (Spring/Summer 2004) and *Readings* (Spring/Summer 2008), that latter of which was directed by the fashion photographer Nick Knight with an original soundtrack courtesy of the musician Antony Hegarty of Antony and the Johnsons. And just as film, and, even more so, music now magnifies fashion's power to the point where it might seem that any celebrity, be they major or minor, can launch a collection with their name printed in the back of it, Chalayan has, conversely, pulled back and become quieter and more deliberately elitist in his approach.

Chalayan's ability to distil the social and cultural issues of the age into desirable clothing is just as finely tuned as it has always been, however. During a three-season partnership with Swarovski, the designer took it upon himself to send mechanical clothing out onto the catwalk. The most startling example of this was, perhaps, the first. *One Hundred and Eleven* (Spring/Summer 2007) was a musing on fashion history featuring models on stage wearing a remotely operated, mechanical dresses that transformed into a variety of styles from one older style into the next more modern form: from prim Victoriana, which fell away to reveal the model's throat and legs, then the skirts of a thirties line column rose thigh-high and, for the awe-inspiring finale, a vaguely futuristic crinoline skirt morphed into a mirrored Space Age shift. The following season (Autumn/Winter 2007), *Airborne* was a no less ambitious exploration of climate change and the cyclical nature of any life force. Chalayan, whose interest in technology was at that point more overt than ever, designed mechanical hoods, light-up headwear and a tunic that displayed a short film. The aforementioned *Readings*, meanwhile, was, Chalayan told me following

Readings, Spring/Summer 2008.
Still from a video directed by Nick Knight.
See 'Disembodiment' p.183.

its screening, an exploration of the origins of our obsession with celebrity culture which, according to the designer, had its roots in ancient cultures' worship of the sun. To express this viewpoint, Chalayan embedded laser technology into crystalline dresses to dazzling effect.

'The lasers point to the crystals first so that they look as though they're glowing,' Chalayan says, 'and then come away from them, creating prisms around the body. I felt that could almost be like the idea of a person emitting light and then light coming back to create those patterns. That, to me, somehow symbolised the process of performing and being admired back. It was almost as if the light was the response from the audience, as if there was an interactive moment of worship.'

As the world changes, and the fashion industry becomes ever more unwieldy and increasingly controlled by faceless corporations, Chalayan is forced to protect his niche more fiercely. The creation of a fashion empire – or even just a single collection – is a costly business and, with no advertising budget or backer, the challenges faced by a designer of Chalayan's level are many. It would, with this in mind, have been only too easy for him to make the sort of compromises that more than a few of his generation have been forced to – or even to decide to move on and do something else entirely. Such an about turn would not be beyond his reach. That, though, is thankfully not in Chalayan's nature.

'Even when I was a child, I really just wanted it my own way or no way,' he says. 'I always rebelled against my parents. If they told me to dress in a certain way I would refuse. I was a free spirit. I felt I had to be that way in order to grow. I'm in it for the long term and in that journey you do sometimes question what you're doing and whether it's worthwhile. I've worked very hard for a long time now and I manage to keep renewing myself. At the end of the day, it's a bit like reading. You read for yourself, you read to learn. And I learn a lot from my processes. It's my choice to do this. I could easily have closed the whole thing down and worked for somebody else but I don't choose to do so. What drives me is this work that you see.'

ABOVE:
The Tangent Flows, 1993.
Photograph by Adrian Wilson.

OPPOSITE:
Process and development images by Hussein Chalayan
for *The Tangent Flows*, 1993.

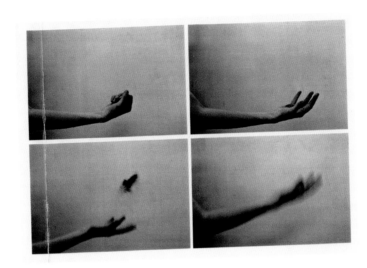

THE TANGENT FLOWS

Central Saint Martins graduation collection, July 1993
The Clapham Grand, Clapham Junction, London

Hussein Chalayan's graduation collection from Central Saint Martins set the ground-work for his intricate creative process. Strictly personal and often biographical, the complex narratives used by Chalayan are powerful tools that assist him in his design approach. For *The Tangent Flows*, Chalayan based his thesis collection on the duality of spirit and matter, researching the works of Isaac Newton and René Descartes, as well as Carl Jung. Chalayan explained his early collection: 'It was about the life of a scientist trying to integrate Eastern philosophy into the Western Cartesian worldview, and the revolts she encountered in her journey. There is a dance which takes place in the story where performers with interactive magnetized clothing (symbolizing the quest of the scientist) have iron filings thrown at them in the form of a protest, they then get kidnapped, murdered and buried with their clothes intact. I then re-enacted this action and buried clothes from this imaginary dance performance with iron filings on them, which later I showed with segments of text from the story relating to what happened to the dancers as labels in the clothes.' Although the narrative systems Chalayan puts into place allow him to release his ideas, he is conscious that as a fashion designer the final result is in clothes. He stated: 'I think processes are there for the designer. The result is the important thing for the people and they don't have to know the process.' *Pamela Golbin.*

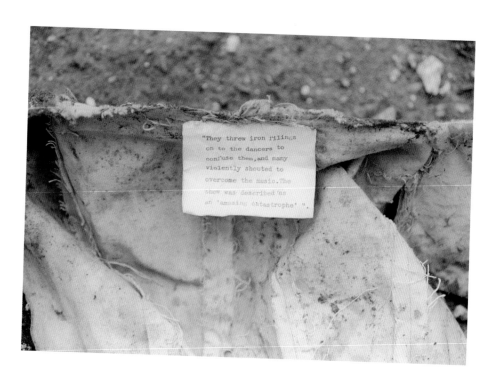

"They threw iron filings on to the dancers to confuse them, and many violently shouted to overcome the music. The show was described as an 'amazing catastrophe'".

HUSSEIN CHALAYAN

Studies and process images by Hussein Chalayan
for *The Tangent Flows*, 1993.
Photographs by Hussein Chalayan.
Model: Sharon Bales.

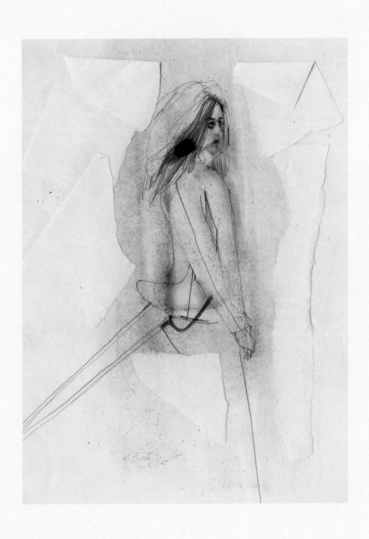

The Tangent Flows, graduation collection, 1993.

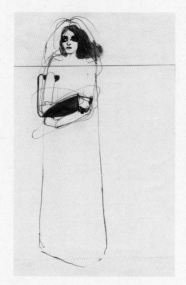
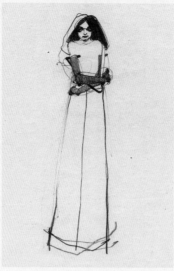

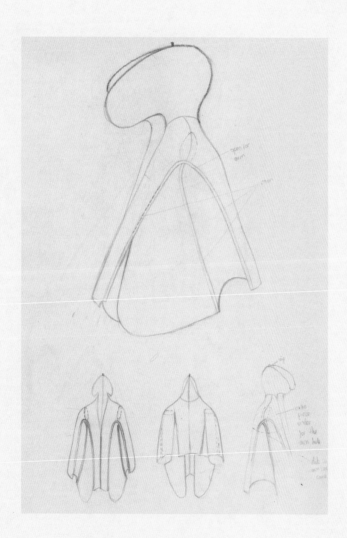

The Tangent Flows, graduation collection, 1993;
student work, 1991 (bottom left).

The Tangent Flows, graduation collection, 1993.

The Tangent Flows, graduation collection, 1993.

The Tangent Flows, 1993.
Photographer unknown.

CARTESIA
Autumn/Winter 1994
Grosvenor Gallery, London, 29 March 1994, 6.00 p.m.

For his first commercial collection, Chalayan developed the narrative of his graduation work, insofar as he remained interested, he said, in Cartesian 'influences over nationalism and fragmentation as an essence of war. The way in which the body becomes anonymous within war. The dead emulated by documents, symbolised by a series of paper garments in contradictory bright celebratory colours, airmail signs illustrating the way in which they could be sent to their places of origin'. He explained his process: 'I used real paper at first. Then I wanted to find something indestructible, so I used Tyvek, which is artificial paper.' Chalayan referenced aerogrammes – which he remembers using in childhood – to create dresses with the airmail letters' distinct folds. The aged and decomposed 'buried dresses' were again presented as an antithesis to the white crisp paper of the *Airmail* clothing. *Pamela Golbin.*

OPPOSITE:
Airmail Jacket from *Cartesia*, Autumn/Winter 1994.
Photograph by Jochen Manz.
Model: Suzanne Lee.

ABOVE:
Cartesia, 1994.
Photographs courtesy Hussein Chalayan and Chris Moore (right).

Björk photographed wearing a Hussein Chalayan
Airmail Jacket for the cover of her 1995 album *Post*.
Photograph by Stéphane Sednaoui.

LOOKING
BACK
ON
HUSSEIN
CHALAYAN

Sarah Mower

Who is Hussein Chalayan, and what makes him design the way he does? I had my first stab at trying to answer that question one morning at the end of 1993, right at the beginning of his career. I thought it would probably take the standard time to rustle up 300 words on a newcomer: 20 minutes on the phone, and goodbye. Actually, it's taken me this long, after innumerable interviews and dozens of shows, to feel I might be getting near the answer to the question. While in school, Chalayan was already gossiped about as the weird Central Saint Martins student who'd embedded his graduate collection with iron filings, buried the clothes, left them to rot and dug them up. This sounded odd enough for me, but when it transpired the young Turkish Cypriot was actually living in a disused vicarage in Crouch End, all that talk of burials and exhumations put me on the alert: student publicity tactics for certain! But no: the lodgings, as it happened, were a coincidence – a doss along the way in an average student life. And the minute he answered the phone, it was obvious this earnest kid wasn't your average desperate graduate whipping up a bit of controversy. I never did get around to nailing my original objective of finding out where, exactly, Chalayan had planted his clothes, and for how long, however, because the second we started talking, he catapulted the conversation straight into the realms of theory.

What he said was something like this, a very Chalayanesque stream of thought I've paraphrased from 1998 interview notes:
'I based it on a story I wrote about a fictional character, who, through a series of performances, tries to connect Cartesian and Eastern philosophies. A theme connected to my thesis about the conflict between the mechanistic worldview and the spiritual worldview. I believe that one of the reasons people don't become interested in studying chemistry or biology is that they can't connect it to the real

Self-portrait by Hussein Chalayan with a disused aircraft
at Nicosia International Airport, Cyprus, 2002.

world. I was interested in how the Cartesian worldview disconnects so many things in our lives that are interconnected.' 'I see,' I said, not seeing at all. 'And your story?' 'It was about a character who, in her attempt to integrate Eastern and Cartesian thought, is subjected to public revolt. For example, in one scene she choreographs a dance. The dancers wear clothes with magnetised panels made to interact with each other, and have iron filings thrown at them by the public as a form of mockery. This then leads to the dancers being kidnapped, killed and buried. I re-enacted this scenario by making clothes from the imaginary dance piece, and burying these clothes with iron filings on them. From all the different scenarios in my story, I placed quotations in the clothes, as labels, to indicate which part of the story they relate to, an attempt to create a sense of life for the clothes.'

I had no idea what he was talking about. Descartes? In a Central Saint Martins thesis – the piece of work most fashion students scrape through with scarcely a thought for punctuation, let alone comparative philosophy? What I did know was this: Hussein Chalayan had come out with a first, and Mrs Burstein, the oracle of the London boutique Browns of South Molton Street, had already selected his rusted iron

filings collection to appear in her windows. The significance of that retail benediction was known to all. It had last been received by John Galliano, straight out of St Martins in 1984, exactly a decade before. The auguries seemed to portend that Hussein Chalayan was becoming 'the new Galliano.'

Except Chalayan was not much like Galliano at all. Even in 1984, it was clear that we – the people of the fashion press – were not going to be able to categorise and explain Hussein Chalayan to our readers in the way we dealt with most designers we'd come across so far. That's quite a big deal, when 'so far' means fashion history to date – enough to make a professional really rather uneasy. A 24-year-old newcomer was threatening to render redundant all the fashion references we critics could call up from our mental hard-drives, which is the way we'd become accustomed to blithely parsing most collections. Whatever this Hussein was up to, it wasn't London as we knew it: it didn't fit the romantic-historicist habit of mind of John Galliano, or the didactic-historic subversiveness of Vivienne Westwood. Nor was Chalayan anything like his contemporary Alexander McQueen – another British lover of narrative history, who rounded the corner from Central Saint Martins the year before Chalayan

and exploded onto the catwalk – except in their shared genius of showmanship. McQueen's work was angry, and macabre, but at least we could understand what it was at a glance.

In the beginning, there was one straw to clutch at. Perhaps that weird *burying* thing meant Chalayan was a new member of the deconstructionist school, following in the footsteps of Martin Margiela and Ann Demeulemeester in Antwerp? Maybe this young Turkish Cypriot upstart would turn out to be part of the contemporary movement which was taking root in Belgium – the thing that was about cutting up clothes, recycling and re-appropriation? That would be neat.

But no. The minute Chalayan actually started showing – messing with our emotions, making us wonder what to make of his work and leaving us feeling completely inadequate to do it justice, without so much as a press release or helpful backstage quote from him – it was clear that we were in new territory. *Uncomfortable, astonishing, poignant, political* and *impenetrable* are some of the words that come welling up when I think of the unforgettable shows he put on in London in the 1990s. The clothes looked clean, scientific and often involved technology, but the main point

always seemed to be not the actual garments but the performance. Once, we sat and watched, entranced as children, as a dress constructed like the fuselage of a plane opened its skirt flaps as if to refuel. Another time, famously, a roomful of models removed chair covers and put them on, turning furnishings into clothes, then filed out, while another model stepped onto the runway and into a hole in a coffee table, arranging the table around her body and wearing it as a skirt.

Watching these events unfold would make the hair stand up on my arms, the visceral sign of a 100 per cent unique fashion experience – sensations for which I thank Hussein Chalayan eternally. It was so clever, so accomplished, so far from operating at the level of trying to change the course of fashion, or bring in the colour red, or appeal to working women or whatever else we expect of a designer. For 20 minutes, Chalayan could lift us out of our trend-chasing rut and make our brains light up in ways we never expected to happen in the course of fashion duty. But just as he would make an entire audience of 500 hardened professionals break into a collective soppy grin of delight, we'd all just stop short, and not catch each other's eyes. Whatever wonderment he was creating for us, it was patently not just for fun and

Temporal Meditations, 2004.
Stills from a film by Hussein Chalayan.

entertainment. What did he mean? What was the subtext? Why did we sense there was so much pain and distress running through these things? Why were we running around saying, 'fabulous, fabulous', when it was so impossible to run back to our computers and explain what Chalayan's work was *about*?

Of course, Chalayan was not the first fashion designer of stature whose work was not easy to make out. We knew what Comme des Garçons was like. We saw how the designer behind that label, Rei Kawakubo, treated clothes as pure form, rather than garments to flatter, and came up with stuff that looked odd, new and difficult – and then she was a difficult designer, too, standing backstage afterwards with one word to offer, if you were lucky. But Chalayan didn't seem to be one of Kawakubo's many acolytes. He didn't seem to want to reinvent clothes quite the way she did, and backstage, he always had plenty of words. The trouble was, we didn't understand them.

The worst time was when, for his Spring/Summer 1998 collection, titled *Between* (which debuted during the 1997 fashion season), Chalayan put on a performance that brought together chadors and nudity. Muslim dress and semi-naked models in one place, shown to a

roomful of outraged women! This, of course, was a show delivered in a world we can hardly remember living in now, two years before 9/11. I felt fear that day. I was afraid that the designer, of whom I'd become fond, would be in real trouble, even danger. But as a feminist I was angry with him. I felt incredibly sorry for the models who'd had to walk onto the runway naked except for face coverings. Had any other designer done that with young girls, we'd have probably walked out and written slash-and-burn reviews afterwards. But no, we stuck around to demand of Chalayan what he was thinking. And this is what we got: 'Well, the whole project wasn't just about the chadors, it was really about how we define our territory culturally, in terms of how we dress. I was really interested in also multiples, how that becomes monumental in a way, how that forms a territory around you and it sort of becomes a different thing. So that's how it started. Then I thought, I wanted to finally juxtapose the cultural and the non-cultural graphic ways in which territory is marked.' Bamboozled again.

Funnily enough, that day Chalayan escaped the nastiest criticism fashion editors are capable of, and even the tabloids, though registering the nudity in a couple of photographs (even they couldn't show the full pubic extent of it) didn't make as much of a scandal of it as they could have done. Because sometimes, even the professionally outspoken don't dare say what they think when they sense they are out of their depth. And Chalayan – by that time an undeniable cultural force, if still a penniless one – was pushing us out of our depth, into a world apparently ruled by art talk, a language we do not speak.

It made for a problem in how we thought of him. Was he being deliberately abstruse and obscurantist, just to tease thick fashion people? Often – sighing and raising their eyebrows as they pushed back through the crowd after shows with notes they couldn't make sense of – journalists suspected it. Very quickly, Chalayan became notorious as one of fashion's more impossible interviews. That did not stop us clamouring at the doors to see his shows: they were some of the most important of the time, and they were thrilling. It's just that, when we had to go back and reduce what Chalayan said (a hopeless task) and what we saw, for our editors and readers to grasp, we were stuck. We needed labels, shorthand for what he did, and so it was that we were left to flail about with whatever blunt instruments were to hand, which, for the purposes of public consumption, had to be the familiar-enough leftovers picked up from decades-old art criticism. We called Hussein Chalayan 'modern', 'minimalist', 'conceptual'. That had to do. Though I always felt that never got to *it*.

One day in 2008, after a decade of trying to ask what made Chalayan different from everyone else, I finally got near the answer on tape: 'My whole thing with fashion was that I wanted it to reflect life. Other disciplines do that. I wanted an all-encompassing approach and through that I would also learn. I wanted to explore and create another perspective', he said. 'I read French cultural theorists: Roland Barthes, Jean Baudrillard. Noam Chomsky is a hero. I always like to read theory. Generally, more and more, I like contradictions, the things we know but can't articulate.'

Aha! That was more like it. It not only explained why his imagery was so hard to pin

down, but made it all right, too. Hussein Chalayan was a poststructuralist, sort of. Perhaps he didn't mind how his work was interpreted, as there could be no one 'correct' view. Then it was OK to look at him, too, from angles he never brought up himself. Even though he was such a loner as a designer, we might also place him in his time, as part of that (in retrospect) weird explosion of hope and artistic creativity which blew up in London around Tony Blair's landslide election in 1997. We could think of Chalayan coming up in the same city, at the same time as the YBAs, alongside the surge of Britpop and Cool Britannia, as one of the agents of change who were making London culture exciting, young and (that very nineties word) *edgy* again.

Chalayan's infamous collection *Between* was shown in 1997, exactly when the *Sensation* exhibition at the Royal Academy of Arts was propelling Damien Hirst's pickled shark, Mark Quinn's *Self* (1991) – a replica of his own head constructed from 4.5 litres of his own frozen blood – and Jake and Dinos Chapman's grisly toy-soldier scenarios onto front pages.

Though Chalayan never went at bloodshed and death as confrontationally as the YBAs, it was there, all right, in the troubling undertow we all detected beneath the calm, technical, sometimes clinical surfaces of his work. In 1997, ethnic tensions in Kosovo had thousands of people leaving their homes, which had reminded Chalayan of what had happened in Cyprus between the late 1950s and 1974. So when we gasped that day in 2000 at the amazing sight of Chalayan's 'family'

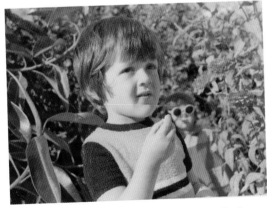

Hussein Chalayan, age five, photographed with his cousin Fetanet in Nicosia, Cyprus, 1975.

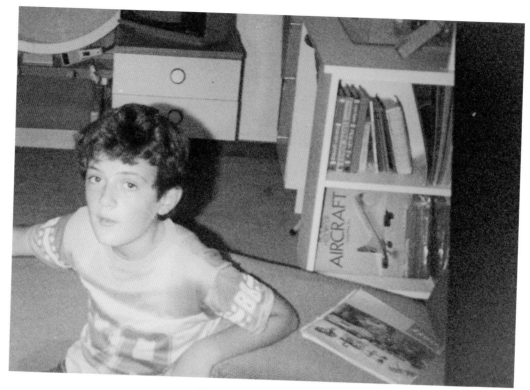

Hussein Chalayan, age 11,
photographed at home in Nicosia, Cyprus, 1981.

of models moving out with their furniture literally on their backs, it was the visual metaphor that made us catch our breath.

And then, we have to record the presence of Alexander McQueen in the same moment. Never a close friend of Chalayan's or the YBAs, either, he was the other significant force in London who was going at fashion as performance, and riveting international audiences. Yet Chalayan and McQueen were so different: fashion's equivalent of Oasis and Blur, slugging it out for attention in the same field. The effect only strengthened London's credibility as a must-visit fashion hotbed. Looked at from an even longer fashion perspective, it was almost like Giorgio Armani and Gianni Versace facing off with their respective stripped-down versus sexed-up aesthetics in Milan in the 1980s. Or Ralph Lauren and Calvin Klein in New York in the 1970s: Lauren pitching classic conservatism against Klein's modernist sensuality.

But we're getting too far away from the thing, which, although not exactly hidden in Chalayan's work, has by far the biggest bearing on his work. As tentative as he is about talking about

the formative influences in his upbringing – something to do with his intellectual intent that the work be seen as an entity somehow distinct from himself, or at least, not literally tied to his life history – it's all there: the reasons behind his fascination with planes, the anxieties about war and religion, the compulsion to research the roots of ethnic identity, the interest in maps and border lines, the fear of being a refugee, the sense of being alone. While little of it is ever overtly dramatised in the finished product, this is Hussein Chalayan's reality, the generator which drives him to 'reflect life', in such a different way from others. Even as his intellect continually sends him outwards into exploring art, architecture, science, medicine, philosophy, ethnography, literature, music, or whatever it may be, all the strongest, most poignant and memorable imagery is linked to his childhood and background. Until the afternoon I got him to sit down and tell the story, I never completely realised the extent of this. For the reams of academic analysis of Chalayan's work that exists, I think all anyone needs to understand him is contained in the following taped conversation.

It begins when he showed me a snap of himself, in his bedroom in Cyprus. Behind him on his shelf is a boy's book on aeroplanes.

Hussein! This book with a Concorde on it, The History of Aircraft. *How old were you in this picture?*

I must be 11. And that's my Lego book behind me.

And where are you?

In my family's house in Nicosia, where my mother and I were living, about 1981. My grandfather kind of designed our living in such a way that we lived in the middle, upstairs was my aunt, below was my uncle, next door was my other uncle, and all the cousins would play all the time.

But what was the political situation in Cyprus, when you were a kid, and when did you become conscious of it?

I was born in 1970. Our community lived in enclaves after the first war [during the conflict between Greek and Turkish Cypriots on the island] in the early 1960s. In 1974, Turkey came in as the guarantor country because we – our Turkish-Cypriot community was being ethnically cleansed and there was a Greek-Cypriot coup in Cyprus threatening to annex Cyprus to Greece. So between 1971 and 1975, I actually lived in London, with my parents in Finchley. My father studied computer programming in the 1960s and then he did Silver Service, and he set up a restaurant business in

Engagement photograph of Hussein Chalayan's father and mother, Ata and Sevil, 1968.

London. Whilst I admire my father, Ata, my mother, Sevil, is my heroine in spirit, creatively and beyond. Then, when I was about five, my parents separated. And so me and my mum went back to Cyprus, we stayed with my grandparents, I went to primary school, but then went back to London for one year again when I was eight, because they wanted me to go to boarding school in Aylesbury, Ashfold it's called.

Eight is really young to go to boarding school, especially in a foreign culture.

It was like a prison. Horrible. I couldn't deal with it, so I went back. I was too young to be away from my mum. Later, I went back and carried on, and came back again when I was 12 until 16. Then I went to the English School back in Cyprus, so really I was back and forth quite a lot. I was there for two years, did my O- and A-levels in two years, because I had to compact it all.

You must have been pretty advanced as a 16 year old to manage that. You told me once it was a very academic education in Cyprus?

Yeah, very good. We see education as our saviour, because it's an island, and isolated, and also because we are politically isolated as well – because we are on what is seen as occupied land; I mean, there was a person killed in every family, for not doing anything, just because we didn't want the island to be united to Greece – so people go out of their way, I think, to get more education as a

Hussein Chalayan's mother, Sevil (above left); Sevil with her elder sister, Sevim, and Chalayan's uncle, Memduh, in Peristerona, now on the Greek side of Cyprus, c.1960.

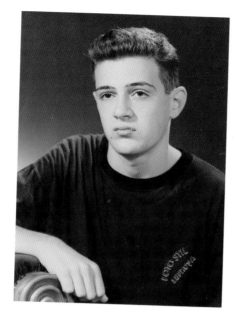

Hussein Chalayan,
Cyprus, c.1986.

way of healing their loss. And in my case, I think
it's also to do with the fact that it's so desolate,
growing up there. I really created my own world.

*What do you mean, 'desolate'? It's a sunny
Mediterranean island, after all.*

I meant there's nothing going on, it's an island.
No cinemas, we watched TV, yes, but we got all
of that from Turkey. It was really just beautiful
and family and food...

That does sound lovely.

I think it does affect the way you also view the
body. I grew up in the sea, so around naked bodies
all the time, waterskiing with my cousin, my aunt's
daughter, Tomur. She had a really big impact on
me. She was a tomboy, the sister I never really had.
She lived above us and she was really feminine,
but she dressed like a boy and I loved that about
her. And all the girls that I always used to like were
like her, like my cousin.

*She's the girl then, the woman we see in your
shows? That figure in your work is a constant.
You don't do sexed-up clothes ever.*

She's my woman, because she was really not girly,
but she was feminine and I loved that contrast,
and she would also be very sporty. She was what
I considered at the time to be very cool.

Unusual girl.

Yes, definitely. It's great that she has followed me
over the years and wears the clothes really well.

*Would Greek-Cypriot children have experienced
a similar upbringing?*

I can't generalise, but they were more affluent,
because they were on the international side, where
there was international investment, tourism.
We couldn't get any of that, so we had a lot less.

*So it was a community that was isolated
and persecuted?*

I think that we were a community that was
persecuted before. The troubles began in the
1960s, when we lived in the enclaves, and we
were third-class citizens. So Turkish Cypriots never
had the same education rights or anything like
that. Ironically, our lives were like a combination
of the experiences of Jews in Europe in the past
and the state of Gaza now. They weren't allowed
in certain places. And then we had an archbishop,
Markarios, as our president. We were not religious,
but they were. So imagine having an archbishop
as your president who was giving one-way tickets
to Turkish Cypriots, to go and live abroad.
As a consequence, terrible things happened to
both communities. But I think we saw 1974 as
our saviour year; we couldn't really give a shit
if we were poorer, because at least we were safe.
Previously, can you believe that my family would
be scared to speak in Turkish in a lot of areas
because that would be frowned upon.

Hussein Chalayan with his grandmother,
Zehra Özel, Cyprus, c.2002.

What impact did your relations' experience of the troubles have on you?

I didn't live through war, but we grew up with the smell of it. There were holes in the walls and many reminders. We lived right behind the Museum of Barbarism, which is a house that was attacked by Greeks; just a house, turned into a museum, where horrific atrocities had taken place. Our garden was adjacent to their garden, so we were always so aware of it. Also, we lived very near the border, which fed this awareness in general.

The Museum of Barbarism? A kind of memorial, next door?

It was a house, someone's house, which was attacked, because our neighbourhood was attacked, it was raided. That's why I did the collection with the chairs, and moving out and all that.

The fear of being a refugee? That show took place three years after what was going on in Kosovo. I see why you felt that so deeply.

In the 1960s my family temporarily had to evacuate their house because they were warned, by someone who knew, that they might get attacked. The family that lived in what has now become the Museum of Barbarism didn't leave. They survived, but with serious injuries. The daughter who had her knee shot out ran a grocery store near our house in Nicosia North. So the remnants of what happened in Cyprus always surrounded us. I grew up going in and out of that grocery store, and that family is a big part of my childhood.

So those recurrent dreads underpin your work? It must have been terribly frightening for an imaginative child.

I remember as a child being so scared there'd be another war that I created this ritual for myself. I'd fold my pyjamas and I'd put them on in a certain way, to avoid war. So I'd create rules for myself. I'd say, 'if I wear the pyjamas this way, it will avoid war', almost like a prayer, kind of like a ritual to avoid war. And one time I remember, I put the pyjamas on the wrong way round and

I panicked there was going to be a war. We were so in fear of it. Then my mum would have these visitors and they would say, 'oh no, there are these orange streaks in the sky… sign of war', and then all night we wouldn't be able to sleep. Especially because of the way people were killed. It was really gruesome, from the stories you heard. In the house next door, there were children and women that were killed, it wasn't just men. So we were surrounded. The remnants, let's say. But it's also really empowering because there's this sort of life-death imminence that you're closer to.

Then on top of all that, you had the stress of flying between two countries and two parents. I always thought the role of flight and aeroplanes in your work emits such a sense of sadness and aloneness – as well your delight in the technology. Even very early on, looking at the airmail envelopes you used as clothing containers and design elements did that. It was such a conceptual appropriation – but you also couldn't help thinking of someone wanting to package themselves up and send themselves somewhere else.

That came from when I used to write letters to my mum, from the idea of longing to be somewhere else, so the garment was a token of that longing. They were beautiful things, those

Airmail Dress, 1999.
Photograph by Matthew Pull.

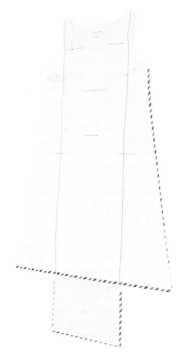

Airmail Dress, 1999.
Photograph by Matthew Pull.

airmail envelopes. I remember writing to my mum when I was eight, at boarding school for the first time. It was very much about the separation of a child and a mother.

In spite of that – just look at those books in your bedroom – you were also excited by the technology and engineering.

I wanted to be a pilot. I used to make model aeroplanes and Phantoms and Lego aeroplanes and towns. The table would become a city, and I would do the announcements on an aeroplane and I would land the aeroplane, and take off, people would come round and we'd create scenarios. Also we were brought up with stories – because the Ottoman Empire had this tradition of children's stories – so my granddad and my grandma always told us stories, and we'd depict those stories, and I would be drawing the characters from these stories doing this and that. I think there's something to be said about being brought up in a place where there isn't too much happening.

But as a child frequent flyer, you can't have associated aeroplanes with untrammelled boyish happiness?

I was really tormented, because I was so happy with my mother, and then my mum remarried when I was 11, you see. My father couldn't stand the idea of me being brought up by a stepdad, so he was just obsessed about getting me over here, and I just really didn't want to come to England. So the aircraft also marked separation for me.

That's what I always thought. It was always double-edged.

But it was the thrill of the flight and the aircraft, too. The thrill and isolation combined, yeah, peculiar that one. I was obsessed with aeroplanes; also having accommodation in them. I was travelling so much back and forth, the idea of an aeroplane having accommodation in it is what sparked the idea of a home that also moved. So it was a home that brought you from one place to another, but regardless it was still a plane.

Inventing these things in your head – and with your hands – did that creativity cancel out the loneliness?

To be honest with you, I was never like, 'Oh my God, I feel sorry for myself!' I never felt sorry for myself, I turned the situation round, and I actually think that I used it in an adventurous way. I love a good adventure. When my father took me away from Cyprus, also because all my family thought I should have a British education, I went to boarding school for a second time, in Highgate. And then, what really saved me was that I drew all the time, drew and drew and drew, and I got art awards and stuff at Highgate before I left at 16 to go back to school in Cyprus.

That constant uprooting: what affect did it have on you?

Part of what happened to me is to do with the fact that I'd been exposed from a very young age to really alien environments that I had to adapt to all the time, and I think that that does affect what I do.

The film you made with the girl in the flying pod captures it all, to me. It was futuristic, but she was so alone and sealed off in her machine. Sci-fi melancholia.

44

That's called *Place to Passage* (2003). It showed a journey from London to Istanbul. The idea is that the vessel becomes like a home to the girl, and she's really sort of displaced to the extent of going back to the womb, so the vessel becomes filled up with water, like a womb.

When you had your premiere, we watched the film in one silent room, and you had a big old noisy Turkish Cypriot barbeque going on in another didn't you?

Yes it was a Turkish barbeque in fact. I got Turks to do it from the East End of London. Because it was such a futuristic film, I thought it was so nice to ground it, by having a barbeque rather than chichi fashion food.

It was really exciting, but, you know, like many things you do, people couldn't fathom it, or make the link between the those two sides of your identity – the convivial Mediterranean side, and then this stark separateness. That girl was very alone.

Well, isolation is a big thing, which is weird, because I'm so social. It's so weird, it's really weird. I know a lot of people, and I love people, in a way, but yet, I am really alone as well, it's peculiar. I think that I'm professionally isolated a bit, because I am a designer who also does other projects and I guess there aren't that many other people who are doing what I'm doing.

What happens is the audience doesn't directly link to the biographical incident, but then somehow the original distress is still there. Which is where you're on the borderline with art, moving beyond fashion.

It's sort of, I guess, a way of dealing with an idea, I guess it's a form of therapy as well, but it's not such a bad thing. It's more that you exorcise it out of you, or something. You're right that there are certain things that are imbued with my background, but also it goes a bit further than that. What happens is that I look also at other scenarios through the emotive, and through, let's say, the historical aspect, and I think that has become, now, a general thing for me.

To me, the most stunning time you used flight was in the show where you had your first mechanical dress – the one built like plane fuselage, where a catch flipped open, as if it was being refuelled. When that happened, people clutched each other with delight. And Audrey Marnay, who wore it, broke into a little seraphic smile.

That show was called *Echoform* (1999). The set was a box and as it opened, there was the sound of the Islamic call to prayer, do you remember? It was at the time of the first Iraqi war. Operation Desert Fox, when the Americans bombed during Ramadan. Audrey became a plane.

It takes my breath away, realising that. At the time it only registered with me as an ingenious performance with an amazing mechanical dress, which amused and astonished everyone. You never spelled out the political comment. Don't you mind that people can just go off with completely the wrong impression? Or have no clue about the synthesis of ideas behind a performance?

It's an experiment about how something can be perceived. I'm like a storyteller in sound and form. I think of it as a world science, but using clothes. I mean, I live in all these co-related worlds I can just slip in and out of. One moment, I'm working with lasers and mechanical dresses, and God knows what – and the next moment, the show's over, and my mother's chasing me with stuffed vine leaves!

It can be quite funny sometimes, the way your layers of meanings can be mistaken. Like when we thought, Oh! Hussein's lightened up – he's done a Hawaiian print with palm trees and ruffles this summer! And then you zoom into the pattern, and it's actually of a battle going on.

It was about the history of Cyprus. Venetians and Ottomans transposed to fighting in modern-day hotels and fields on the borders of Nicosia.

It's not just history you research. Science, too.

A look from *Temporal Meditations*, Spring/Summer 2004, exhibited at Istanbul Modern, Turkey, 15 July to 24 October 2010. Photograph by Fatih Metin Demirkol.

You got interested in DNA at one point.

I was trying to find out what Cyprus DNA is. I had myself tested, and found out all kinds of things – one being that I have a Viking gene, from when they came down through Russia, via my father, and another the Cambridge reference, the most common European gene, from my mother. There is a Byzantine strain. Look at my face – it's like what you see in a Byzantine mosaic! It's all super-duper mixed. What's interesting is not where you came from though, but the story of how you got there.

I still think that your work has an emotion in it, which really puts people on edge. It just makes people sense there's more there, even though it's not totally apparent. I wanted to ask more about being from a Muslim background. You have gone into controversial religious territory, but you were a secular community in Cyprus?

Turkey is secular; Cyprus is even more secular. If you see anyone veiled now in Cyprus, they're from Eastern Turkey, they're not from Istanbul or big cities, even though the scarf is a political not a spiritual symbol. So no, it's super-secular. No one had ever been to a mosque in their lives, it's not really part of our upbringing. But of course the dominant religion is Islam, even in a secular setting.

OK, let's talk about the chador show [Between, Spring/Summer 1998]. Wouldn't your female family members have been completely shocked by that? Because you shocked a lot of women...

Oh, my aunt, we call her Bette Midler, because she looks like her, have you ever seen her with my mum, blond? Her and my mum – my cousin Tomur imitates them really well – after the show, everyone had left, and them two were just sitting there looking like... statues. You have to remember that I did that before this whole Islamic controversy. I was shitting myself, I don't know how the hell I got the guts to do this, because I was worried for a start that the girls might freak, because we had to convince them and convince them and convince them.

It involved actual nudity and religion, why?

Why did I do it? It was about how we define our territory culturally, in terms of how we dress. I was really interested in the idea of multiples: if I saw five other people wearing the same thing, how that becomes monumental in a way, how that forms a territory around you. That's how it started. In another section I wanted to represent the graphic way in which someone can define their territory, so it's actually not cultural, and then mixed the two. I had these dresses that were pinched from the middle of the torso, or from the side of the body, which I would allow to drop as a frame drape to mark negative space around the body. To redefine the cultural codes, I looked at South American religious attire and made these square head-dresses, which framed faces. And finally I wanted to look at the chador, and thought, well, they're trying to be anonymous, but actually it has the reverse effect. It was imbued with so many ideas, such as nurture and nature. You are born nude and, through this cultural conditioning, you become like a mummy in a sense. And then of course, it was controversial because it's a chador. When I see a covered woman I think it's like a floating body, where identity is suspended.

What about the importance of staging, performance and music in your work? It's so intrinsic to you. When did that kind of theatrical thinking start?

Actually, it's interesting, because I wanted to become an actor in my teens. I had a cousin, Misli, who was an actress and grew up in Canada, a third cousin, who influenced me a great deal. She also influenced me later, introducing me – at age 11 or 12 – to listening to Grace Jones. No one in my school liked Grace Jones. They all thought she looked like a man and couldn't sing. I was interested in movement and the body, and music was really connected to this. I was listening to a lot of stuff that maybe my contemporaries weren't listening to, and I think I was connecting music to form even at that age – you dress in the way that you listen to music. My hair was shaved and I had just one bit of hair at the front... I was into everything post-punk. Music was really empowering for me, but my interest in performance stemmed from my interest in art. In my late teens, I would see a lot of stuff, and, I thought, why not introduce this way of thinking into fashion? Even at St Martins, my graduation show was a bit like a performance. At the end of the day, whatever is said, for me it's all about perception. And I guess all the things I've been exposed to, including cultural clashes, have greatly contributed to this.

But, now having made this leap, from you being a well-educated, intellectual, creative boy, to going into fashion.

Well, I always drew women wearing clothes, always. It's to do with me being around women, and the empowerment of women, because my mum was a single mum, and it really stood out. And obviously I thought, I guess, it was to do with giving that situation power. My mum also, I have to say, with my aunt, made her own clothes and they were really advanced at the time, and no one's mum made clothes like that. They really had good taste then. She wouldn't just make them, she'd drape – so I always saw her making stuff, cutting patterns. Also, they'd make patterns from magazines, as well, adjusting them. I remember my mum walking in a fashion show, for God's sake, in Cyprus in the 1980s. She'd wear these long gowns with a split, and she was taller than the other girls. They were really into it.

Did you help?

No, but I was around it. Actually maybe – no, I didn't help, but I was interested, definitely. But, of course, you didn't want to be seen to be a sissy.

Clearly you've been creating and making things since you were a child.

You see the desk in that photo in my bedroom? I had actually designed this piece of furniture myself – which was unusual then, because it's a desk, but it also has a bookcase on the side. I was like, 'Oh my God, that's amazing, I can get that made!' I made a lot of things, with wood and other

materials, we'd constantly make things. I would unpick machines, take them apart and do stuff with them. I just tampered with things all the time.

How did you get to art school and then Central Saint Martins?

I had been really good at art at school. When I was 18 I went to Mid-Warwickshire College and then to Central Saint Martins in London. My maternal grandfather helped me out at the time, he was so happy when I got a first [-class degree] from Central Saint Martins.

But here's the thing, Hussein: I always wondered, whether, with all your interests, intellectual capabilities, your mind for everything from engineering to abstract music – and your ability to make things – haven't you gone wrong somewhere? Shouldn't you have been an architect, interior designer, theatre or movie director, scientist or philosopher, instead of someone who has to make a living out of selling clothes?

Well I think that would've been boring. The point is that I'm applying that all to clothing and that is what makes the work, I think, more interesting. The way I look at fashion, I treat it as a world science.

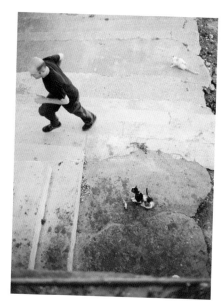

Hussein Chalayan, North Cyprus, 2002.
Photographs by Mark Borthwick.

TRANSCENDENCE

SPEED AND MOTION

METAMORPHOSIS

BLIND SPOTS

DISEMBODIMENT

NEW ANTHROPOLOGY

MIGRATION

TRANSCENDENCE

The thoughts expressed by music are not too vague to be put into words, but too precise. – Felix Mendelssohn

IDEAS about transcendence pervade and inform Hussein Chalayan's entire body of work. The immaterial and the harsh and fast reality of fashion do not obviously go together – quite the opposite – and so it is interesting that he should be so concerned about what might be beyond fashion or what may lie out of its natural reach. It is made more interesting given the (Western) sociological claims that one cannot ever be truly outside the fashion system in the way that we might not be able to be outside the knowable world. In attempting to transcend the fashion system Chalayan has appealed to the efficient symbolism of allegorical and religious representation – the work of making the unknowable visible.

He has wondered what it might be to venture vertically, an axis less travelled by designers. Things happen above us in our poetic imagination. Religious iconography tells us that it is from above, from the sky, that we receive illumination and inspiration.

Chalayan's kind of storytelling comes through collections made up of sequential designs, creating narratives akin to the episodic fresco, though we do not expect them, today, to follow the narrative of biblical or evangelical canon – even though these have always incorporated dressed figures.

His is never an overtly religious project but one that seems to want to hunt for representations of invisible forces, be they religious, ecstatic or gravitational, and how these representations may be both worn and performed within the controlled environment of the catwalk. How might one perform ideas of Fate, Death, or irreversible Time itself? And what does it mean to place a coffin or a clock on a stage, or a trampoline? How high can we go?

Light, used conventionally to spotlight the models on the catwalk, and in doing so to create the important divide between performance and audience, is used both metaphorically and as a pun by Chalayan. Light stands in for enlightenment and the Enlightenment, for passion, a saintly aura as well as that of the new celebrity. His use of tiny LED lights woven into the fabric of a gown have themselves become a decorative language, like the dashboard in front of an air traffic controller. Chalayan's might also be 'light' as in the opposite of heavy, which works in two ways – something that floats heavenly, and something that is after all not so serious.

He has also used light to enact absence: he has made jackets that were made out of a photoluminescent rubber that stores light and then glows in the dark. His models were hugged in bright light backstage, in order that when they walked out they glowed with a human imprint and revealed their absence. Bodies that are usually revealed under light become floating visions if their heads and hands are in darkness. Powerfully linked to ideas about disembodiment and at least in his early work aggressively anti-overt sexualization of his designs.

Body and mind or body and desire can be in two places at once. Chalayan's alter ego, or counterpart, can live separately, sometimes in the idea of an afterlife and sometimes the fantasy of a virtual second life.

In *Ventriloquy* (Spring/Summer 2009) an alter ego was enacted by an avatar in a film about dissolving morality at the time of catastrophe. Alter egos were created as caricatures, and turned into Japanese manga cartoon-like animations – a virtual environment void of social and moral structure. In a lecture at the Architectural Association in 2000, Chalayan explained:

It was like creating a visual poem where everything was exaggerated. What was interesting to me was the interplay between this [film] and what happened in the live/performance event. Sugar-glass dresses were created, so when they were smashed they could react, shatter, as their surrogates on screen had a few moments earlier. So they are wearable but breakable.

Death appears at the end wrapped into the folds of the skirts as fabric printed with poppy fields so immediately evocative of post-war mourning, like the inaudible words of a lament. *Judith Clark*

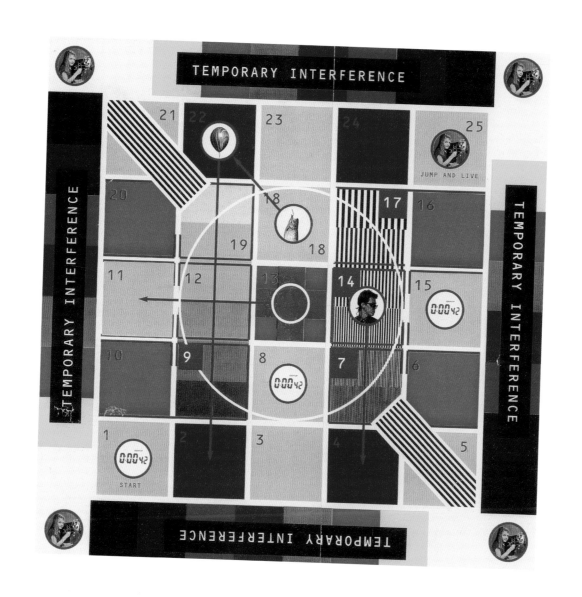

TEMPORARY INTERFERENCE
Spring/Summer 1995
British Fashion Council Tent, Natural History Museum, London,
9 October 1994, 6.15 p.m.

For *Temporary Interference*, Chalayan created a board game (above) in which the notion of God as the weather interferes temporarily with our daily lives. The designer said: 'It was a fictional game... about the hierarchy of God and man and about how we see God as a separate entity. That for me is Cartesian philosophy.' The act of throwing the dice controlled what would happen to the clothes. Whatever direction one took in the game, the result was always that one had to jump off a great height in order to reach the Divine. The balloons worn by the models were to assist in their ascension to the heavens, but they inevitably fell short of their destination symbolizing, for Chalayan, the fallacies of religion and its contradictions as well as the 'absurdity demonstrated by jumping off bridge heights in the hope of being saved by an exterior force'. 'Buried dresses' are shown in various states of decomposition after falling from flight into a river, or more symbolically, after falling from grace. *Pamela Golbin.*

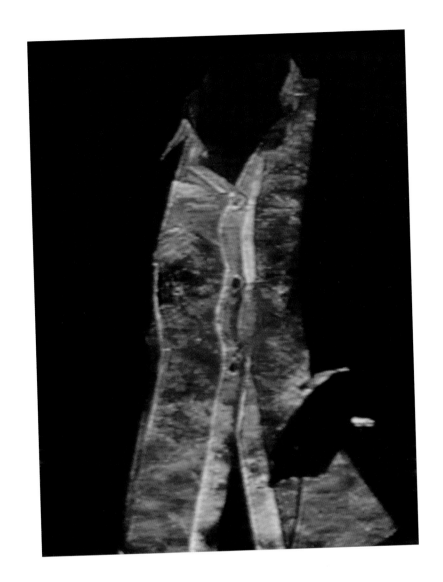

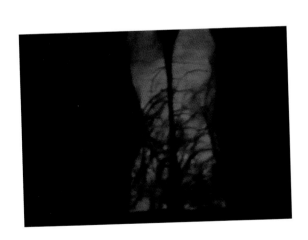

Temporary Interference, Spring/Summer 1995.
Show photographs by Chris Moore.

ABOVE:
Temporary Interference, Spring/Summer 1995.
Show photograph by Chris Moore.
Model: Rebecca Lowthorpe.

OPPOSITE:
Flight-path patterns drawn for
Along False Equator, Autumn/Winter 1995.
Image courtesy Hussein Chalayan.

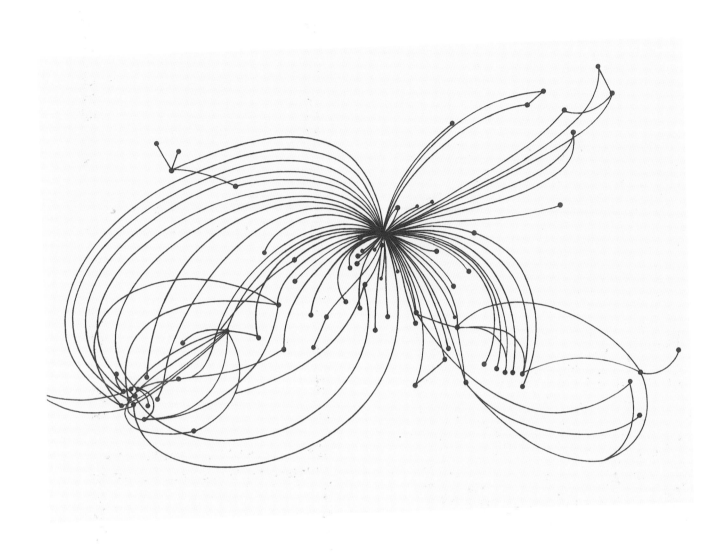

ALONG FALSE EQUATOR
Autumn/Winter 1995
British Fashion Council Tent, National History Museum, London,
12 March 1995, 6.30 p.m.

Airline routes, cardiograms, meteorological charts and photographic landscapes are all used as prints and decorative elements in this collection which explored the notion of being in transit while simultaneously being omnipresent. Chalayan uses 'travel as a means of exploring the external world and the world within'. LED lights represented flashing airport lights. Flight paths printed onto the clothes created an atlas embodying a sense of constant movement. Printed neoprene (the material used in scuba diving clothes) evoked a change of environment and the urgency of an aeroplane's takeoff. At a time when globalisation issues were just beginning to emerge, Chalayan explored travel as a means of attaining ubiquity since the body can physically be anywhere, a state that he described as, 'an inhuman mechanic materiality that can tear away your skin'. *Pamela Golbin.*

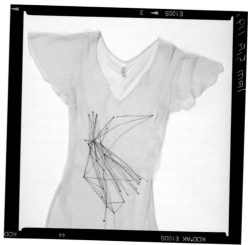

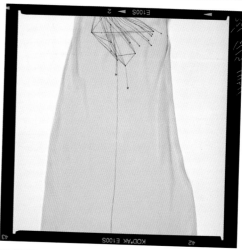

ABOVE LEFT:
Marie Claire magazine (UK), September 1995.
LED jacket photographed by Troy Word.

ABOVE RIGHT:
Along False Equator, Autumn/Winter 1995.
Photographs by Katarina Jebb.

Along False Equator, Autumn/Winter 1995.
Show photographs by Chris Moore.

Along False Equator, Autumn/Winter 1995.
Show photographs by Chris Moore.
Models: Rebecca Lowthorpe (top and right) and Tabitha Simmons (left).

SCENT OF TEMPESTS

Autumn/Winter 1997
Atlantis Gallery, London, 27 February 1997, 4.30 p.m.

For Chalayan, *Scent of Tempests* inaugurated a new chapter in his design process, in which his narrative became more abstract as he attempted to create a wardrobe in relation to a religious belief system. 'Often I find that people who worship pray for bad things not to happen,' Chalayan observed. *Scent of Tempests* warns of an impending disaster, an explosion in the waiting. After designing his collection *Temporary Interference* (Spring/Summer 1995), external forces were again incarnated by the weather. In *Scent of Tempests* this took the form a god that was part of nature, punctuating our daily lives. The designer's intention was to create appropriate attire for worship. Although the jewellery in the collection could have Islamic connotations, Chalayan used it as a decorative element to adorn the devotee in his veneration just as the embroidered fans – which were also part of the collection – served to embellish and protect the wearer. *Pamela Golbin.*

ABOVE:
Scent of Tempests, Autumn/Winter 1997.
Show photographs by Chris Moore.

PAGE 61:
i-D magazine, October 1998.
Stills from a video by Donald Christie.

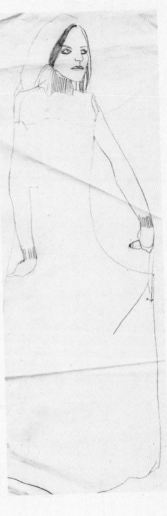

Scent of Tempests, Autumn/Winter 1997.

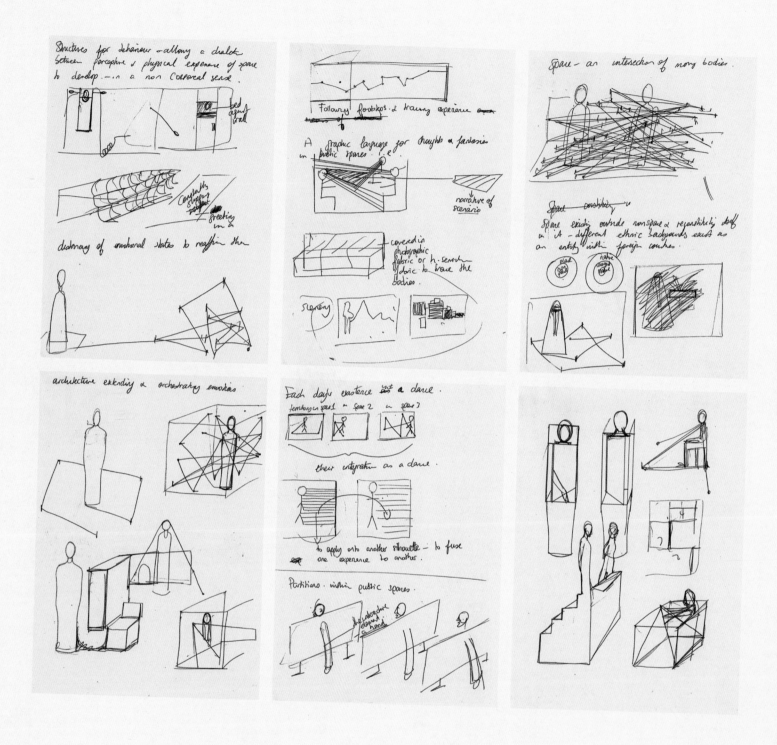

Between, Spring/Summer 1998.

Between, Spring/Summer 1998.

Between, Spring/Summer 1998.

BETWEEN

Spring/Summer 1998
Atlantis Gallery, London, 27 September 1997, 8.15 p.m.

A natural continuation of *Scents of Tempest*, the collection *Between* further explored the notion of worship and deconstructed how we define our territory through belief systems. During the creative process of designing the collection, Chalayan asked nude models to stake out an area on a beach in Dungeness, East Sussex, using ropes and poles, thus defining their territory. Once the physical space was marked out, Chalayan explored and questioned the notion of identity which can easily be erased by the concealment of one's face. Models dressed in red wore egg-shaped capsules that entirely covered their faces, offering a certain protection from the gaze of others but completely removing any sense of their individuality and eliminating their personality. Others wore headpieces framed in mirrors that allowed the spectators to see and be seen in their reflection. The show ended with six models dressed in black chadors of varying lengths. The first walked out completely naked, wearing only a minute yashmak that hid her face. The following models wore chadors that increasingly concealed their nude bodies. Controversial but not confrontational, Chalayan was interested in showing how through 'the religious code you are depersonified.' *Pamela Golbin.*

Between, Spring/Summer 1998.
Photographs at Dungeness by Donald Christie for Hussein Chalayan.

OPPOSITE:
Süddeutsche Zeitung Magazin, 20 February 1998.
Photograph by Horst Diekgerdes.

ABOVE:
Between, Spring/Summer 1998.
Show photographs by Chris Moore.

Between, Spring/Summer 1998.
Show photographs by Chris Moore.

THESE AND THE FOLLOWING PAGES:
Between, Spring/Summer 1998.
Show photographs by Chris Moore.

69

VENTRILOQUY

Spring/Summer 2001
Gainsborough Studios, London, 27 September 2000, 8.00 p.m.

Held in a studio where Alfred Hitchcock shot several feature films, *Ventriloquy* began with a computer-animated film (still above, by Me Company) in which a 3D female figure (delineated in wire-frame-like lines) ruthlessly shatters another figure into thousands of pieces, to reflect, Chalayan said, 'how value systems collapse at times of war'. After this virtual interaction, the real models appeared on a white set with a geometrical grid that echoed the one in the animated film. From the chaos of destruction and to music provided by the Jupiter Orchestra, conducted by Gregory Rose, emerged a silhouette of spare topstitched suits, loose shift dresses and intricately pleated, voluminous skirts. Prints of red poppies alluded not only to the flowers' distinctive attribute of thriving in difficult environments but also to their use as a symbol commemorating soldiers killed in action. In the dramatic finale of the presentation, Chalayan sent out six models. Three of them held small mallets with which they smashed their companions' fragile sugar-glass garments, exposing their stark nakedness and mirroring the actions of their alter egos seen previously in the film by Chalayan. *Pamela Golbin.*

Ventriloquy, Spring/Summer 2001.

Medea, Spring/Summer 2002.

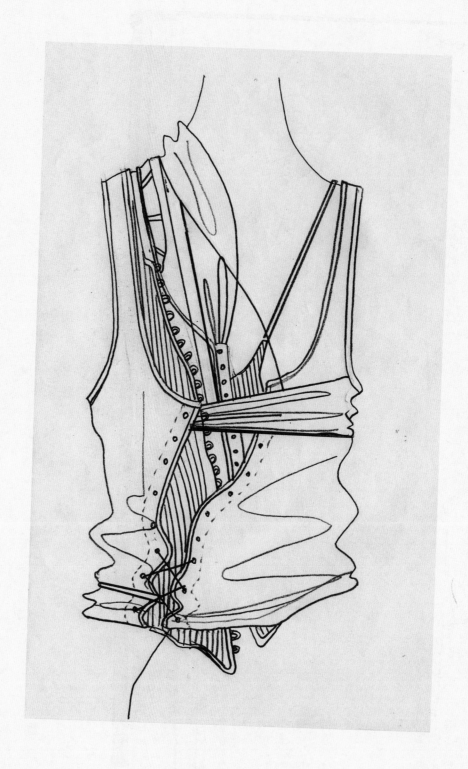

Medea, Spring/Summer 2002.

VENTRILOQUY ⌣

73

PAGE 72:
Moulds for sugar-glass dresses.
Photographs by Lone Sigurdsson.

ABOVE:
Ventriloquy, Spring/Summer 2001.
Show photographs by Chris Moore.

UNIVERSITY OF WINCHESTER
LIBRARY

Ventriloquy, Spring/Summer 2001.
Show photographs by Chris Moore.

MEDEA

Spring/Summer 2002
Couvent des Cordeliers, Paris, 5 October 2001, 8.00 p.m.

Inspired by a *Dictionary of Superstition*, Chalayan uses the sorceress Medea and her magical powers as the central figure of this collection. 'The design is a wish or a curse that casts the garment and its wearer in a time warp through historical periods, like a sudden tumble through the sediment of an archaeological dig,' Chalayan explained. Through elaborate seaming and detailing, the garments were built up in various layers of silks and cottons. They have been deconstructed, sometimes tattered, twisted and ripped to represent the wishes and/or curses. Thus, the altered conditions of the garments symbolize a hexed state. 'The garment is a ghost of all the multiple lives it may have had,' Chalayan continued. 'Nothing is shiny and new; everything has a history... Thus a 1960s dress gets cut-away to reveal its past as a medieval dress; or, in reverse, a Victorian corset gets cut away to reveal a modern jersey vest; a 1930s dress gets cut away to disclose its past as an Edwardian dress.' As a *clin d'oeil* to the work presented at his college graduation show, Chalayan buried and aged some of the dresses of the finale. *Pamela Golbin.*

THESE AND THE FOLLOWING PAGES:
Medea, Spring/Summer 2002.
Show photographs by Chris Moore.
Models: Stella Tennant (opposite, left) and Erin O'Connor (above, top left).

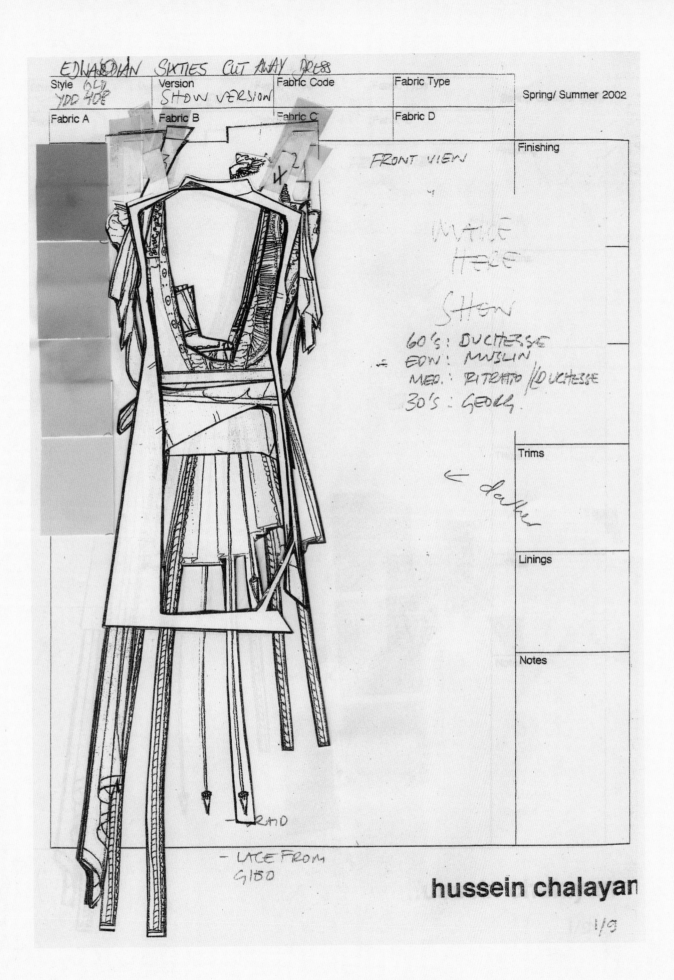

EDWARDIAN SIXTIES CUT AWAY DRESS

Style (LD) YDD 408	Version SHOW VERSION	Fabric Code	Fabric Type	Spring/ Summer 2002
Fabric A	Fabric B	Fabric C	Fabric D	

FRONT VIEW

Finishing

IMAGE
HERE
SHOW

60's: DUCHESSE
EDW: MUSLIN
MED.: RITRATTO / DUCHESSE
30's: GEORG.

Trims

← darker

Linings

Notes

— BRAID

— LACE FROM
GIBO

hussein chalayan

1/9

Medea, Spring/Summer 2002.

Kinship Journeys, Autumn/Winter 2003.

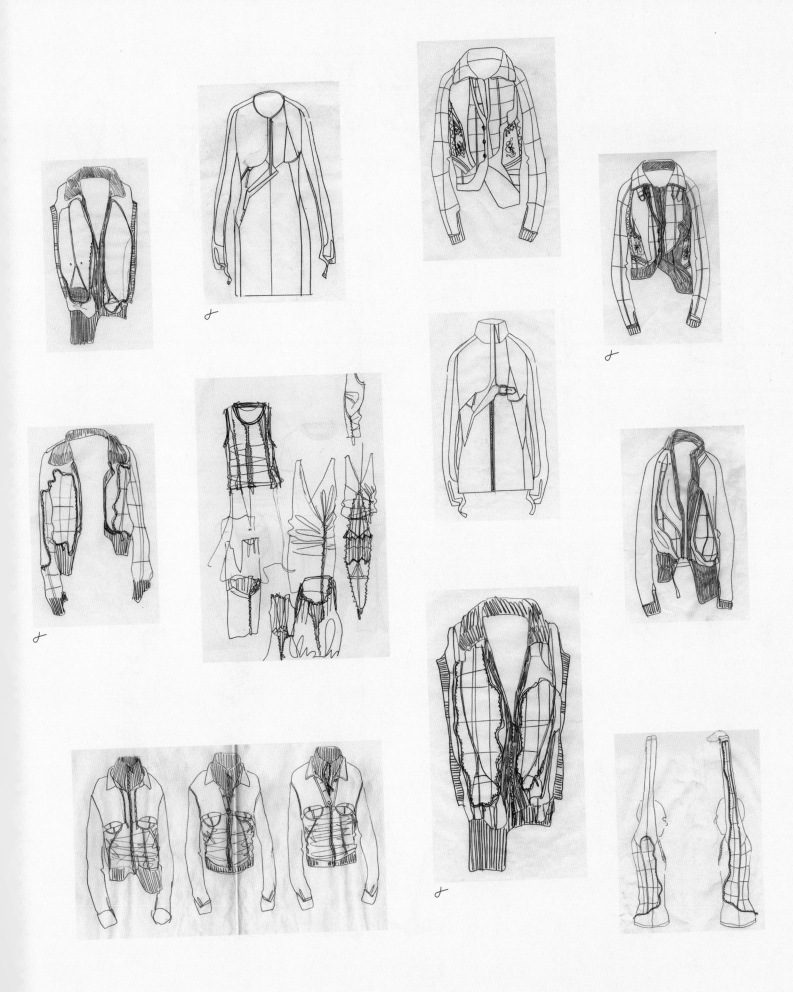

Kinship Journeys, Autumn/Winter 2003.

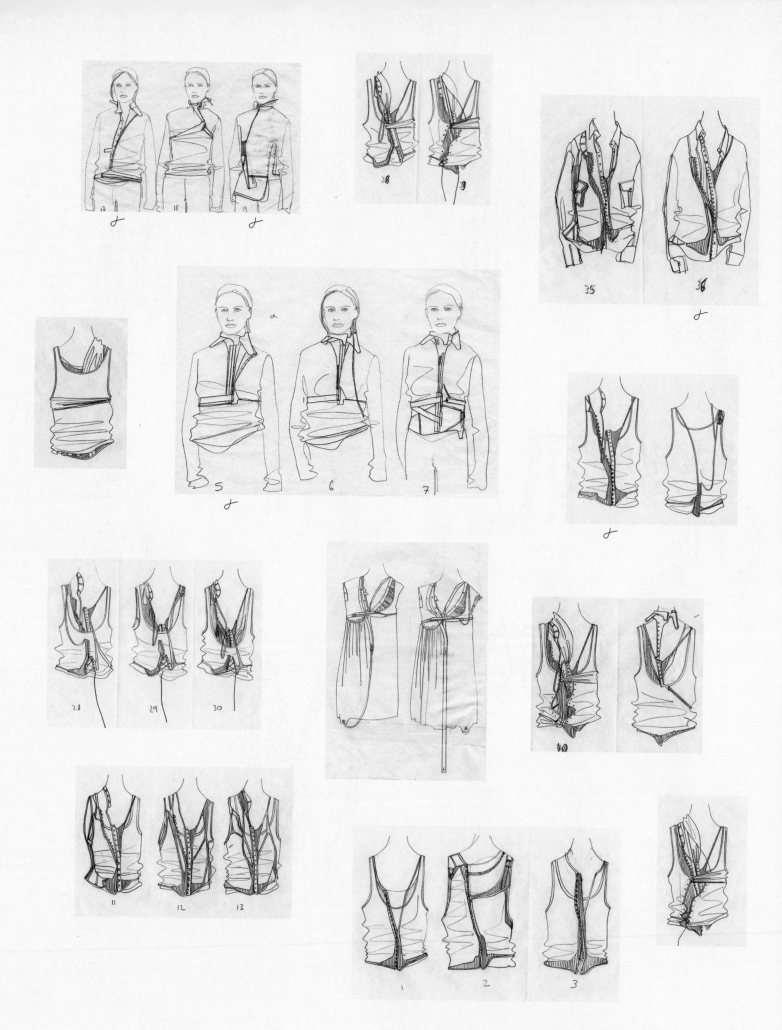

Medea, Spring/Summer 2002.

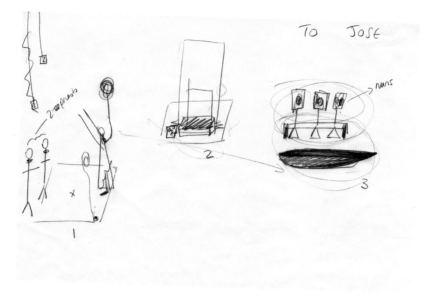

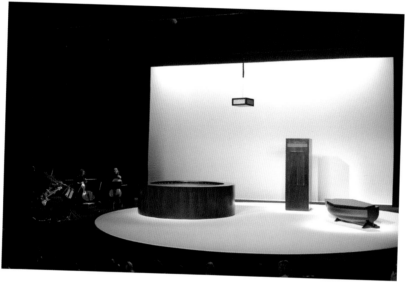

KINSHIP JOURNEYS
Autumn/Winter 2003
Théâtre de Paris, Paris, 7 March 2003, 8.30 p.m.

With *Kinship Journeys*, Chalayan commented on the practices of the Roman Catholic church and the meaning of hope, sin and salvation in our lives. Chalayan explained: 'The collection was in three parts, each monument on stage related to each section. The first part (the trampoline) represented the idea of trying to reach the divine with the balloons attached to dresses as if they were to enhance the upward movement. The second part represented the way in which we allow our sins and guilt to rule our lives. Hence, after your confession you would plant a seed within a drawer of the confessional that contained soil and your sins would manifest themselves as fruit or flowers. The final part, evolving around the coffin boat and (eventually) buoyant clothing, is perhaps a comment on resisting death.' First presented by Chalayan in his Spring/Summer 1995 collection, suspended balloons were used as an artifice to elevate the model to the 'Divine' for a deliverance that will not occur. Dresses, jackets and coats were built up through abstract layering of plaid and military camouflage motifs. Fragments of embroidered olive branch patterns were inspired by Turkish folk costume. *Pamela Golbin.*

Kinship Journeys, Autumn/Winter 2003.
Show photographs by Chris Moore.

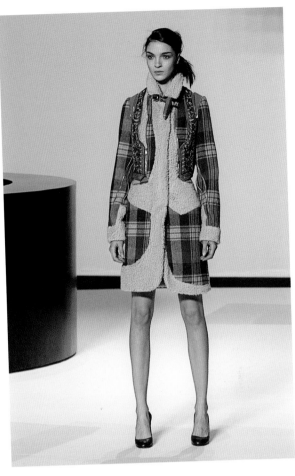

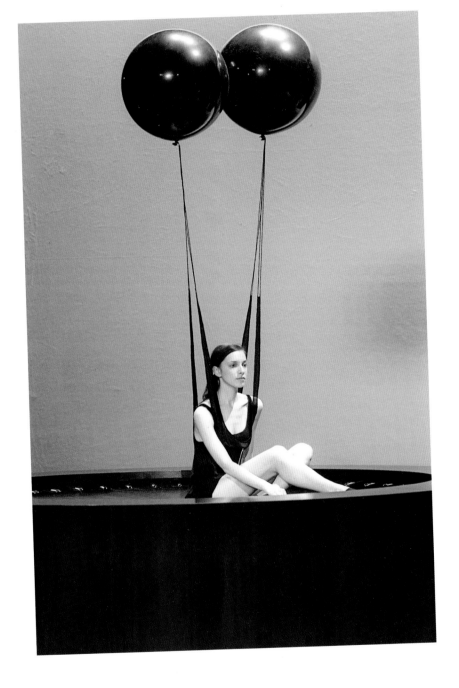

OPPOSITE:
Pop magazine, 2003.
Photograph by Peter Lindbergh.

ABOVE AND THE FOLLOWING PAGES:
Kinship Journeys, Autumn/Winter 2003.
Show photograph by Chris Moore.

ABSENT PRESENCE

2005
A film written and directed by Hussein Chalayan,
screened in the Turkish Pavilion at the 51st Venice Biennale

This 13-minute film explores, Chalayan explained, 'the neurosis and paranoia around the issue of terrorism and the consequential suspicion of foreign individuals and the British government's "hard line" policies on immigration and asylum seekers.' The narrative followed non-British, female, anonymous donors whose DNA sequences were extracted from their clothing by a biologist played by actress Tilda Swinton. New garments were generated from the donors' clothing through an animated scene in which the DNA sequences were mapped onto the London soundscape. The clothing morphed according to the presumed sensitivities of each donor. Photograph (above right) by Thierry Bal.

TRANSCENDENCE

SPEED AND MOTION

METAMORPHOSIS

BLIND SPOTS

DISEMBODIMENT

NEW ANTHROPOLOGY

MIGRATION

SPEED AND MOTION

THOUGH Hussein Chalayan is universally claimed as fashion's futurist, conjuring images of aerodynamic invention and transformation, he is just as likely to stage a romantic gesture; such as a model raising and lowering her arms as if flying like a bird – as he is to build a remote-controlled *Aeroplane Dress*. He does not fix definitions of his work despite it being so apparently laden with meaning and intention. His version of flight always encompasses both the wonderful freedom of exploration – free from earthbound, national boundaries – and that of taking flight from imminent danger.

The Futurists' early 20th-century cry for a progressive, technological world created an idiom from which Chalayan could draw aesthetically: streamlined cars and aeroplanes, for example. These references were far enough from the history of dress such that they could return to haunt his designs, a powerfully and interestingly corruptive force: it was dress itself that could become the chink in the armour of modernism.

The clean lines of modernism become, in Chalayan's work, a perfect counterpoint to the intricate detailing and colour of non-Western local dress creating an idiosyncrasy quite different to Futurism's goals. Chalyan proves that a sense of place can be quite literally sewn into the journey. Dress can also stand in for movement, shifts in the landscape: incremental shifts in the detailing of a dress, layering, adding or subtracting enacted within the quasi-mathematical encoding of a fashion collection.

The compositional logic of Chalayan's most extreme 'monuments' – as the designer refers to significant pieces that express the central theme of a show and are often the finale, such as the *Aeroplane Dress* and the *Remote-control Dress* (1999–2000), both of which are mechanical – is ironically not involved with the mobility of the body (in fact, sometimes Chalayan's designs seem more about *immobility*) and so Chalayan's fantasy, counter to that of Futurism's, is not entirely involved with enhancing the body's power and speed.

Always allegorical, Chalayan's fibreglass dresses surrender their control, in effect, to a little boy holding a remote control, or the digital editing of Marcus Tomlinson's films, or the show production of Chalayan's long-time collaborator Alex de Betak.

Movement was one of Futurism's defining themes, and, as a theme in Chalayan's projects, movement is embedded in both the material and structure of his garments. Whereas early 20th-century painters depicted movement frozen in space as multiple blurred outlines, Chalayan might sew multiple seams along his hems – but they are not the reinforced seams of a *tuta*, but instead the hem of a refugee's cape – movement represented, movement imposed and movement enacted.

Speed is to do with travel, and like a camera zooming in and out of a view of the globe from space, the scale of Chalayan's journeys changes dramatically. If you are far enough away you can see the picture. Speed can be the dramatic impact of a car crash, or the slow erosion of a mountainscape. Chalayan's glorious pink tulle 'topiary' dresses – as they are often called – do not in fact refer to the whimsical frenzy of an Edward Scissorhands figure, but instead refer to the result of natural erosion, the impact of the weather over time. It is always the intangible forces at work that grip Chalayan's imagination. The impact of the moon's gravitational forces or the idea of technologically enhanced speed creating a violent mark: its impact is its imprint and on the dress, a print.

The elegant lines of stealth craft that were overt in earlier collections have, over time, become simply the seams into which a more classical drapery is hinged. Technology changed within Chalayan's work from muse to methodology, aesthetic to tool. Chalayan describes this process as 'internalising' his references: it is as though they now go underground in the service of the dress, dress that is allowed for the first time recently to be overtly sexy.
Judith Clark

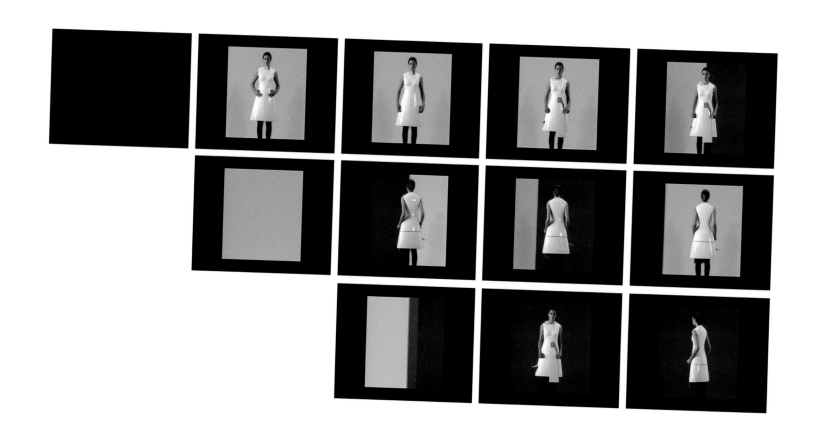

ECHOFORM
Autumn/Winter 1999
Playscape Go-Kart Centre, London, 24 February 1999, 7.30 p.m.

For his last three collections, Chalayan has explored the definition of barriers, whether physical, linguistic or geographical. With *Echoform*, Chalayan probed the notion of speed and its relation to the body – whether it is used to propel the body forward through technological advances or as a reflective force. 'Everything we do is an amplification of the body,' Chalayan noted recently. 'And I thought why not look at those things and then project them back onto the body.' Cars and aeroplanes were the direct inspiration for the collection, materializing the man-made machines that best symbolize speed. Chairs, headrests and streamlining were integrated into the structure of the garments. Leather padded headrests or neck cushions accessorised the dresses and echoed the forms from which they are derived. Chalayan presented a second version of his *Aeroplane Dress* made of fibreglass and resin cast into an aircraft form. Operated electronically, the skirt integrated flaps that can extend just like the wings of a plane. *Pamela Golbin.*

Aeroplane Dress, Autumn/Winter 1999.
Photographs by Marcus Tomlinson.

ABOVE:
Echoform, Autumn/Winter 1999.
Show photograph by Chris Moore.
Model: Audrey Marnay.

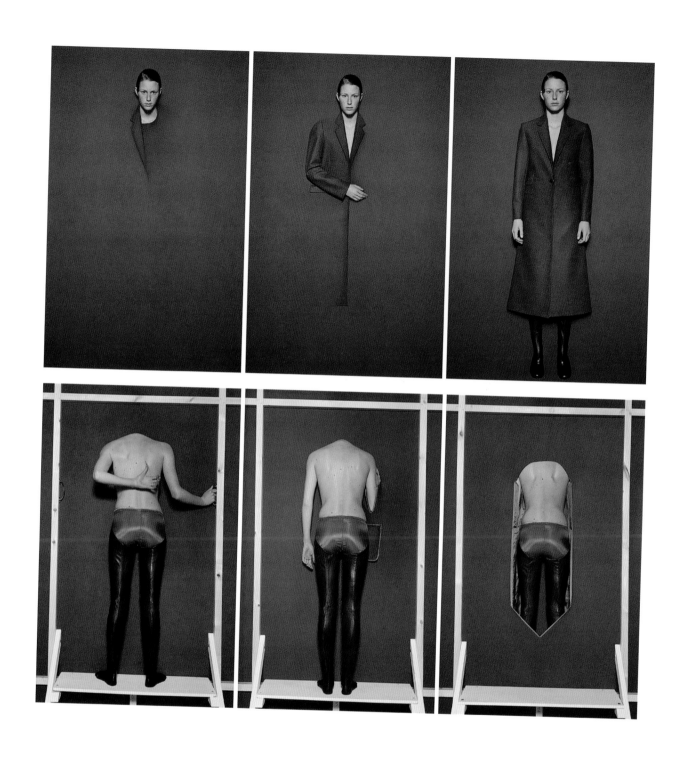

Frame, 1999.
Photographs by Marcus Tomlinson.

  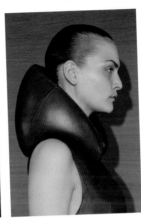  

Reduction Room, 1999.
Photographs by Marcus Tomlinson.

BEFORE MINUS NOW
Spring/Summer 2000
Sadler's Wells Theatre, London, 23 September 1999, 8.00 p.m.

In *Before Minus Now*, Chalayan focused on invisible forces as a means to construct form. The designer was particularly interested in phenomena that become visible entities. He explored the powers of expansion, magnetism and erosion and how these can be applied to garments in order to create shape. To express expansion, Chalayan used heat to modify the shape of a flared red dress. Harking back to the 1950s New Look silhouette, Chalayan's take on the feminine dress was inflated on stage where it unfolded and amplified in volume. Then, Chalayan's fibreglass, remote-control *Aeroplane Dress* was transformed with the touch of a button. The body was consequently metamorphosed through an artificial, man-made force that combined the elements of magnetism and technological advances. To embody the action of erosion, Chalayan shaved a bale of shapeless pink tulle giving it the contour of a dress. In the same way that the formation of mountains occurs through natural erosion, Chalayan formed his own monuments through the gradual cutting of the fabric. In the finale, five models were presented, wearing deconstructed corsets in vivid colours with matching pleated skirts. With these designs, Chalayan paid tribute to the natural force of the wind as a powerful tool that can alter and create forms. *Pamela Golbin.*

OPPOSITE:
Jalouse magazine, March 2000.
Photograph by Barnaby Roper & Scott Lyon.

ABOVE:
Vogue magazine (US), 2000.
Photograph by Mario Testino. Model: Kate Moss.

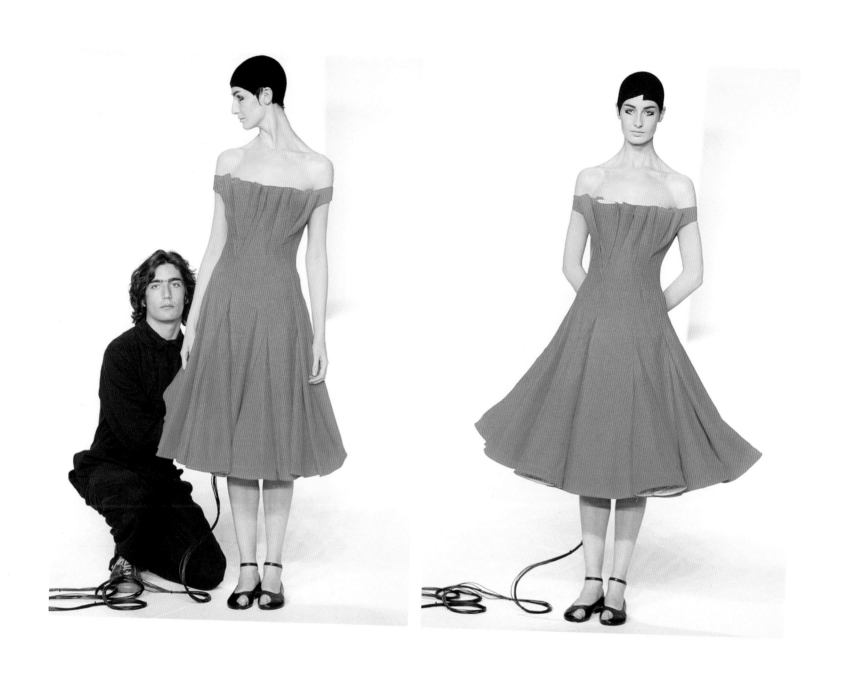

Before Minus Now, Spring/Summer 2000.
Show photographs by Chris Moore.
Model (above): Erin O'Connor.

Before Minus Now, Spring/Summer 2000.
Show photographs by Chris Moore.

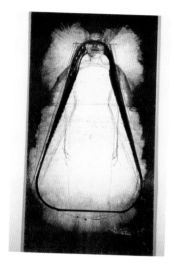
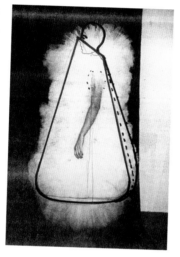

ABOVE:
Working sketches by Hussein Chalayan
for *Before Minus Now*, Spring/Summer 2000.

OPPOSITE:
Before Minus Now, Spring/Summer 2000.
Show photograph by Chris Moore.
Model: Erin O'Connor.

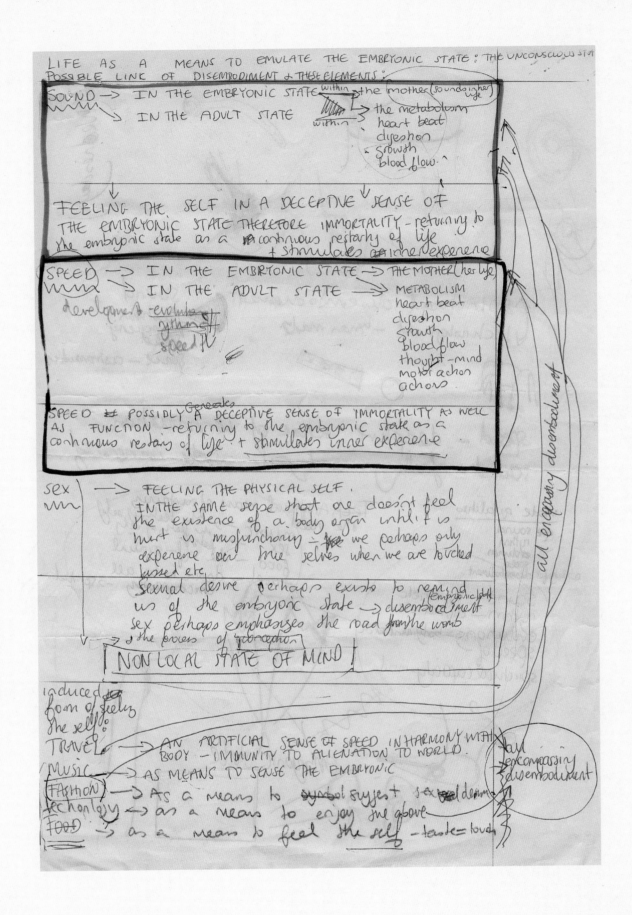

LIFE AS A MEANS TO EMULATE THE EMBRYONIC STATE: THE UNCONSCIOUS STA
POSSIBLE LINE OF DISEMBODIMENT & THESE ELEMENTS:

SOUND → IN THE EMBRYONIC STATE within → the mother (sound is her life)
→ IN THE ADULT STATE within → the metabolism
heart beat
digestion
growth
blood flow.

FEELING THE SELF IN A DECEPTIVE SENSE OF
THE EMBRYONIC STATE THEREFORE IMMORTALITY - returning to
the embryonic state as a continuous restarting of life
+ stimulates inner experience

SPEED → IN THE EMBRYONIC STATE → THE MOTHER (her life)
→ IN THE ADULT STATE → METABOLISM
heart beat
digestion
growth
blood flow
thought - mind
motor action
actions.

development - evolution
rhythm
speed

SPEED POSSIBLY A DECEPTIVE SENSE OF IMMORTALITY AS WELL
AS FUNCTION - returning to the embryonic state as a
continuous restart of life + stimulates inner experience

SEX → FEELING THE PHYSICAL SELF.
IN THE SAME sense that one doesn't feel
the existence of a body organ until it is
hurt is misfunctioning - we perhaps only
experience our true selves when we are touched
kissed etc.
Sexual desire perhaps exists to remind
us of the embryonic state → disembodiment (embryonic state)
sex perhaps emphasizes the road from the womb
+ the process of conception

NON LOCAL STATE OF MIND

induced
form of feeling
the self:

TRAVEL → AN ARTIFICIAL SENSE OF SPEED IN HARMONY WITH
BODY - IMMUNITY TO ALIENATION TO WORLD.
MUSIC → AS MEANS TO SENSE THE EMBRYONIC
FASHION → As a means to suggest sex death
technology → as a means to enjoy the above
FOOD → as a means to feel the self - taste = touch

all encompassing disembodiment

all encompassing disembodiment

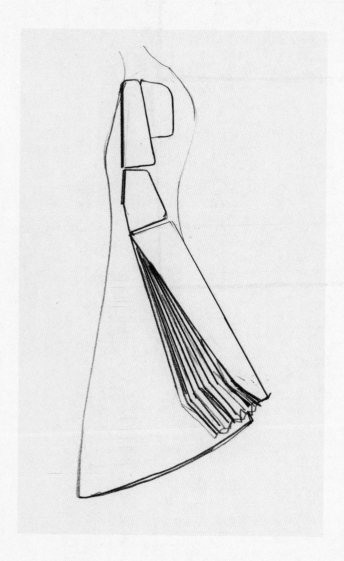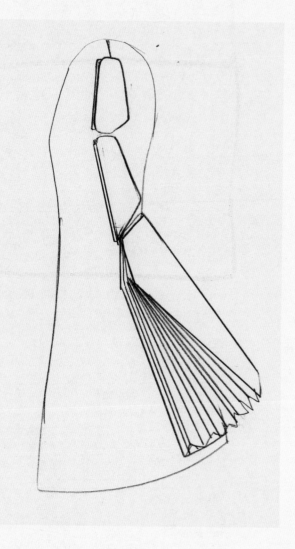

Before Minus Now, Spring/Summer 2000.

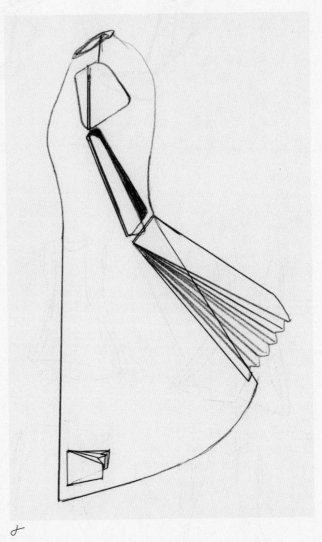

Before Minus Now, Spring/Summer 2000.

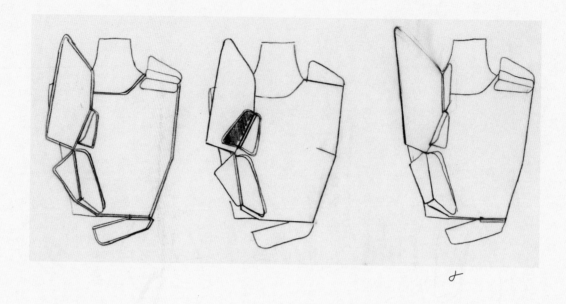

Before Minus Now, Spring/Summer 2000.

Before Minus Now, Spring/Summer 2000.
Show photographs by Chris Moore.

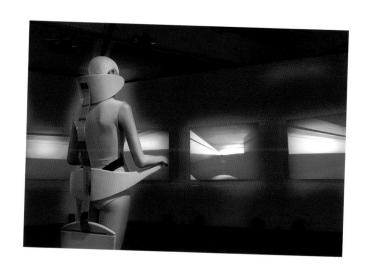

PLACE TO PASSAGE
2003
A film written and directed by Hussein Chalayan, commissioned by Tribe Art and premiered at The Truman Brewery, London, October 2003

After a visit to the B.A.R. Honda Formula One racing team, Chalayan was moved to create his own fantasy version of a racing car. Borrowing the team's modelling techniques, Chalayan built what he termed 'an aerodynamic pod-like structure,' which was the focus of this five-screen installation featuring Bennu Gerede, seen above at Istanbul Modern (2010, photograph by Fatih Metin Demirkol). The pod's occupant, Chalayan explained, was 'an androgynous female passenger who has created an imaginary living space where temporary refuge, memories of another life, isolation, nostalgia and exploration all merge into one.' She is carried through a surreal landscape, from London to Istanbul, ending at the Bosphorus River, which delineates the boundary of Asia and Europe. The pod ended its journey in an underground parking structure, which Chalayan stated 'symbolically marks both the end, and the start, of a new journey'.

REPOSE
Autumn/Winter 2006
Carrousel du Louvre, Paris, 1 March 2006, 12 p.m.

Through *Repose*, Chalayan continued to explore the notions of travel and movement. Whereas in his collection *Echoform*, Chalayan presented neck cushions and an *Aeroplane Dress* as a metaphor for speed, with *Repose* he mixed in a domestic reference. Household furniture elements were incorporated into the silhouettes to combine travel with a domestic setting. Wood-grain-printed dévoré silks, exaggerated neck lines – reminiscent of gentlemen's club chairs – patterned seat covers and Victorian upholstery allude to the comfort of the home. The state of the body may be in movement but the accoutrements of a comfortable sedentary life were ingrained in these designs. After the stormy dreams presented in *Blindscape* (Spring/Summer 2005), *Repose* offered a restful pause. *Pamela Golbin.*

ABOVE:
BigSHOW magazine, Autumn/Winter 2006.
Photograph by Warren Du Preez
and Nick Thornton Jones.

OPPOSITE:
Repose, Autumn/Winter 2006.
Show photographs by Chris Moore.

REPOSE

2006

An installation by Hussein Chalayan for
Swarovski Crystal Palace and the Kunsthalle Mannheim

Repose, a conceptual art installation, featuring specially cut crystals, was commissioned by Swarovski in 2006 for the crystal manufacturer's Crystal Palace exhibition at the Salone Internazionale del Mobile, Milan, and additionally for the Kunstalle Mannheim in Germany. Inspired by the concept of flight, Chalayan's impetus for this installation was his view of 'airports as borders, and the physical divide between his own Turkish Cypriot heritage and his life in London'. This installation consisted of an aircraft wing mounted so it extends from the wall. The wing has a large flap which moves up and down to expose a strip of illuminated Swarovski crystals, lit from behind by LED lights. Chalayan has explained the piece: 'A single seat folding out from the wall, with a passenger sitting outside the aircraft, represents absurdity, excitement and experience of flying, manifesting itself as an out of body experience.' A version of *Repose* has been purchased for permanent display by Istanbul Modern.

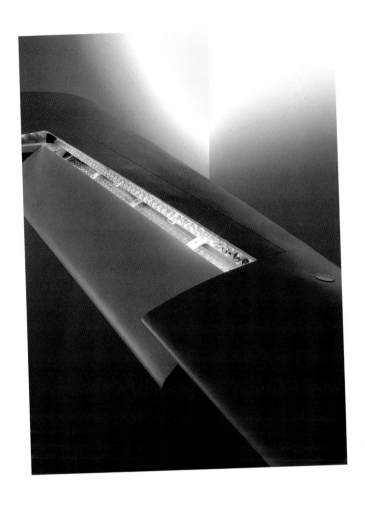

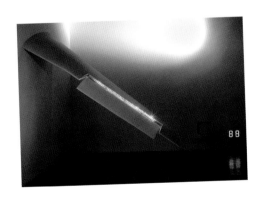

OPPOSITE:
Repose, 2006, installed at the Museum of Contemporary Art,
Tokyo, 3 April to 20 June 2010.
Photograph by Keizo Kioku.

ABOVE:
Repose, 2006, installed at Swarovski Crystal Palace,
Salone Internazionale del Mobile, Milan.
Photographs courtesy Hussein Chalayan.

INERTIA

Spring/Summer 2009
Palais Omnisport de Bercy, Paris, 1 October 2008, 7.30 p.m.

The concept of speed was the focus of this collection. Chalayan noted: 'Speed has become the essence of all facets of how we live our lives today, where daily processes are speeded up to achieve as much as possible in the quickest possible time... The crash represents the result of this fast-paced living and of the ever-growing emergency. The corset reference represents therapy. It is the idea that the pieces (of the body) are held together via these surgical corsets.' Envisioned as three sequences, *Inertia* employed images of 'body cavities' and 'car graves' printed on bonded jersey with foam edging in metallic grey and Porsche red. Organic forms in the silhouettes' construction symbolized the natural world which was overtaken by violent images of broken windscreens, embellished embroideries and rubber edging. 'Finally,' Chalayan added, 'the body became the "event" of a crash where garments caught in the midst of speed simultaneously embodied the cause and effect of a crash in one moment.' With the live smashing of dozens of glasses lined up in a bar inset, the finale brought together five models frozen in motion on a revolving podium wearing spectacular molded latex mini-dresses hand-painted with images of crashed automobiles. *Pamela Golbin.*

OPPOSITE:
Studio development collage for
Inertia, Spring/Summer 2009.

ABOVE:
Inertia, Spring/Summer 2009.
Show photographs by Chris Moore.

THESE AND THE FOLLOWING PAGES:
Inertia, Spring/Summer 2009.
Show photographs by Chris Moore.

ABOVE:
Inertia, Spring/Summer 2009.
Show photograph by Chris Moore.

OPPOSITE LEFT:
B-Side, Spring Projects, London, 2010.
Photographs by Noah Da Costa, courtesy Spring Projects.

OPPOSITE RIGHT:
Poster image for the exhibition *Hussein Chalayan:*
From Fashion and Back, London, 2009.
Photograph courtesy Hussein Chalayan.

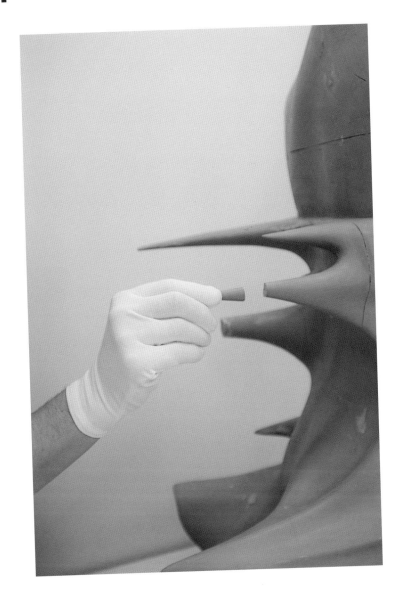

B-SIDE

An installation by Hussein Chalayan,
Spring Projects, London, 17 September to 23 October 2010

This installation was a grouping of two discrete projects, *Anaesthetics* and *Inertia*, which together articulate Chalayan's key themes. *Anaesthetics* consisted of the 2004 film that was previously screened at the Moderna Museet, Stockholm, and The 21st Century Museum of Contemporary Art, Kanazawa, Japan. For this installation, light boxes displaying stills from the film and three-dimensional objects were debuted. *Inertia* was the title of Chalayan's Spring/Summer 2009 collection. He chose to give insight into his clothing-making process by showing moulds that were used to create rubber foam dresses for that collection. Chalayan stated that not only were the moulds beautiful, but that showing the moulds were about 'the monumenatalisation of the frozen moment'.

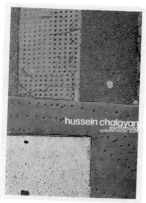    

EARTHBOUND
Autumn/Winter 2009
Couvent des Cordeliers, Paris, 8 March 2009, 3.00 p.m.

Earthbound was inspired by changing environments, the desire to stay routed amidst a constant state of flux and the way in which even the development of our architectural landscape can be indicative of the body's gradual development. Chalayan used architecture, building processes and building materials to translate the urban London landscape into clothing. He wrote: 'Concrete foundations are evoked through specially developed bonded grey puffa, whilst sculptural fabric in fine black, white and grey weave is worked into organically draped mini-dresses, which suggest concrete in its flowing liquid state. A photographic print of grey asphalt pavement moves the concept from foundations to ground level and adds texture... Finally, bright turquoise and coral embellished prints of scaffolding and stone move into a section of specially created, vibrantly coloured moulded leather busts and bottoms attached to soft concrete-print leather dresses. These elements are incorporated to create the impression of architecture, blurring the gap between reality and fantasy.' *Pamela Golbin.*

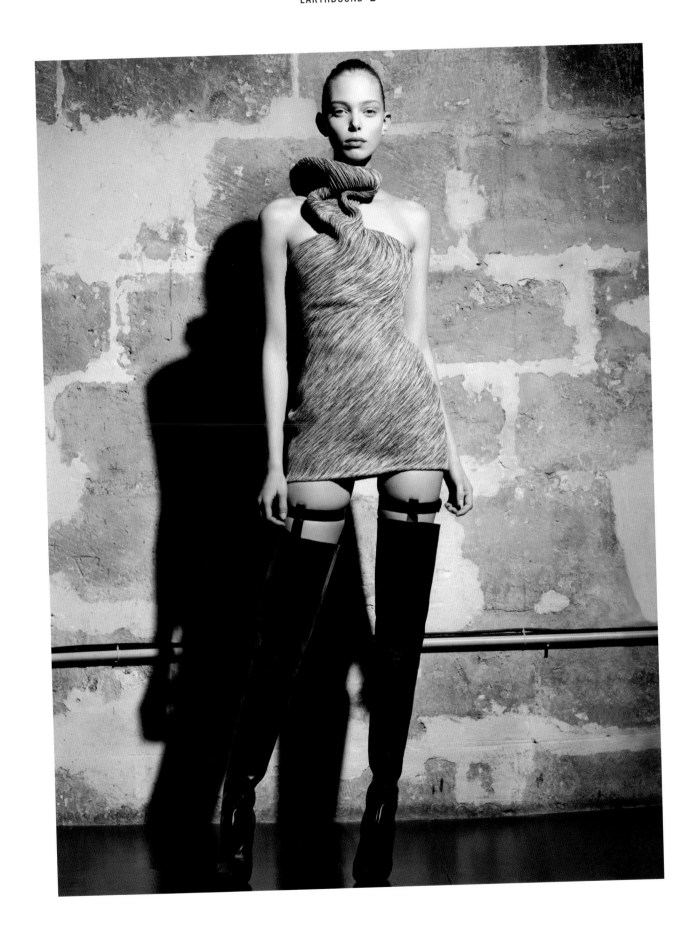

OPPOSITE AND ABOVE:
The lookbook for *Earthbound*, Autumn/Winter 2009.
Photographs by Amy Troost. Model: Tanya D.

119

Earthbound, Autumn/Winter 2009.
Show photographs by Chris Moore.

Earthbound, Autumn/Winter 2009.
Show photographs by Chris Moore.

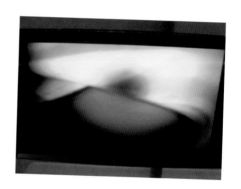

MICRO GEOGRAPHY – A CROSS-SECTION
An installation by Hussein Chalayan,
Museum Boijmans Van Beuningen, Rotterdam,
19 September 2009 to 10 January 2010

Micro Geography – A Cross-Section was an installation consisting of a glass observation box with a rotating human figure in the centre, dressed in one of Chalayan's designs. Chalayan described it as 'a gelatin-like space which eradicates all sense of distance and remote experience.' Adjacent video screens displayed close up images. Exploring themes central to Chalayan's work – technology, nature, omnipresence, voyeurism and new anthropology – the piece, he explained, 'represents the grandeur of collective experiences... and is a reaction to how experiences are spread out and how we are constantly moving around.' Photographs (above) by Hans Wilshut.

TRANSCENDENCE

SPEED AND MOTION

METAMORPHOSIS

BLIND SPOTS

DISEMBODIMENT

NEW ANTHROPOLOGY

MIGRATION

METAMORPHOSIS

METAMORPHOSIS is both change and evolution: the evolution of fashion or that of a single dress, but also of Man, both past and future. Chalayan's references range from Stone Age flint fastenings (reminding us of our common origins) to sartorial evolution, as in his Spring/Summer 2007 collection *One Hundred and Eleven*, in which a model wore a mechanical gown that 'performed' the history of fashion, suggesting the stylistic trends of one decade after another (making clear that the dress is the idea). Sometimes in Chalayan's work an external object merges with the model's body creating a body-sofa or body-plane or body-wall, but that seems almost too literal to be Chalayan's definition of metamorphoses.

In Chalayan's hands dresses can enact the fashion system itself, with its mutating hemlines and quickly morphing silhouettes: dresses equipped with battery packs, controlling chips and minutely geared motors directing every change. The choreographed dress. The dress that zips itself – even that most mundane of actions is rendered magical.

Mario Perniola's now seminal essay 'Between Clothing and Nudity' published in the journal *Zone* in 1989*, claimed: 'Eroticism appears as a relationship between clothing and nudity. Therefore, it is conditional on the possibility of movement – transit – from one state to other. If either one of these poles takes on primary or essential significance to the exclusion of the other, then the possibility of transit is sacrificed, and with it the conditions for eroticism. In such cases, either clothing or nudity becomes an absolute value.' There is something of this in Chalayan's work – if a dress were just a dress, or rather complete as a dress, or had no transformational story, it would cease to be so captivating. It is why the formula of the catwalk and the collection work so well for Chalayan: as it is through sequences that Perniola's famous transit can be acted out.

Chalayan's work is never collage – we can never see the place where a reference was cut out or conversely stuck on. Chalayan does not use nudity as the erotic component; instead, by introducing an alien idea, the whole body becomes erotically charged. There is always a dynamic aspect to the clothes, he gives them a life of their own, their own trajectory, 'as though they have come through something, or been somewhere before', he often repeats. Something has always lingered and something is always yearned for.

Chalayan recreates again and again the dilemma of place and destination: of tradition reconfigured gradually for a modern self, of body towards its robotic other, of East to West. One collection for Spring/Summer 1999, *Geotropics* (see 'Migration', p. 231) imagined a journey along the Silk Route: the flat lines of a kimono were digitally morphed with the darted, gathered bias of Western dress along the way. Animation is important to Chalayan, not so he can get a perfectly constructed picture, but for the minute control that it provides to capture in-between moments within the plot. A millionth of a second is, for Chalayan, Perniola's moment of transit; the possibility of being in two places at once.

Chalayan's process can be metamorphosis as well. The rubbing out of an idea is somehow recorded in the layering of the next. He takes the evolution of his own thoughts, his own process, very seriously. His graph paper and scribbles allow uncertainty into his designs. Traces of one design linger, and are projected onto the next as though the dresses themselves had developed a kind of memory. *Judith Clark*

*Mario Perniola, 'Between Clothing and Nudity,' in *Zone 4: Fragments for a History of the Human Body*, Part 2, eds. Michel Feher, Ramona Naddaff and Nadia Tazi (New York: Zone Books, 1989), 237.

AMBIMORPHOUS

Autumn/Winter 2002
Cité de la Musique, Paris, 8 March 2002, 9.00 p.m.

In Chalayan's 2003 statement for his Mode Museum, Antwerp, exhibition, the designer explained: 'The aim of this project is to explore the shady territory between realism and surrealism, power and powerlessness. As an example, I intend to examine the connections between *Alice in Wonderland* as a representation of a surreal entity, and war as a real life force.' To illustrate his theme of power and powerlessness, Chalayan's models walked out through props of differing scales, to make them seem oversize on one end of the runway and diminutive on the other. He began the show by sending out a lone Asian model dressed in a richly embroidered traditional costume from Western Turkey. Other models followed wearing designs with 'ethnic' detailing as increasingly black coloured 'Western' skirts and pantsuits completely usurped the original costume. The morphing then was reversed. From all-black silhouettes, the ethnic detailing once again was slowly integrated, and the last piece was the costume that began the show. 'The clothes represent forms that are so-called "ambimorphous" where all forms can morph in two different directions...' *Pamela Golbin.*

OPPOSITE:
Ambimorphous, Autumn/Winter 2002.
Photograph by Marcus Tomlinson.

ABOVE:
V magazine, September/October 2002.
Photograph by Peter Lindbergh.
Model: Zuzana Macasova.

Vogue magazine (FR), August 2002.
Photograph by Nathaniel Goldberg.
Model: Karolina Kurkova.

Ambimorphous, Autumn/Winter 2002.
Show photographs by Chris Moore.

ONE HUNDRED AND ELEVEN
Spring/Summer 2007
Palais Omnisport de Bercy, Paris, 4 October 2006, 6.00 p.m.

Chalayan is inspired by the way in which world events, including wars, revolutions, political and social changes have shaped fashion over the course of a century. Through *One hundred and Eleven*, he commented on time and history in a collaboration with Swarovski that celebrated the crystal company's IIIth anniversary. As early as 2001, Chalayan had begun to explore the concept of morphing in his film for the *Mapreading* (Autumn/Winter 2001) collection. With *One Hundred and Eleven*, he pushed the idea further, creating a series of hand-constructed mechanical dresses which, as parts moved, physically morphed from one era's style to another. Representing a fashion history retrospective of over a century, Chalayan began with a high-necked, full-length Victorian silhouette dating from 1895 that metamorphosed, at the touch of a button, to a looser-fitting dress that rose to the calf in a 1910 style before transforming into a distinctive 1920s flapper dress. With six morphing dresses, Chalayan lept through decades and iconic silhouettes engineering a spectacular vision of fashion and its vocabulary. The soundtrack provided a contrast to the stunning technological feats by bringing together audio fragments taken from jet engines, trench warfare and aerial bombings. *Pamela Golbin.*

One Hundred and Eleven, Spring/Summer 2007.
Show photographs by Chris Moore.

ABOVE:
One Hundred and Eleven, Spring/Summer 2007.
Show photographs by Chris Moore.

OPPOSITE:
BigSHOW magazine, Spring/Summer 2007.
Photograph by Warren Du Preez and Nick Thornton Jones.
Model: Morgane.

ABOVE:
One Hundred and Eleven, Spring/Summer 2007.
Show photographs by Chris Moore.

OPPOSITE:
Rehearsal for *One Hundred and Eleven*, Spring/Summer 2007.
BigSHOW magazine, Spring/Summer 2007.
Photograph by Mischa Richter.

FOLLOWING PAGES:
BigSHOW magazine, Spring/Summer 2007.
Photograph by Warren Du Preez and Nick Thornton Jones.
Model: Morgane.

ABOVE:
One Hundred and Eleven, Spring/Summer 2007.
Show photographs by Chris Moore.

OPPOSITE:
Inner workings of mechanical dresses from
One Hundred and Eleven, Spring/Summer 2007.
Photographs by Adam Wright (mechanical designer).

OPPOSITE, BOTTOM LEFT:
Backstage at *One Hundred and Eleven*, Spring/Summer 2007.
BigSHOW magazine, Spring/Summer 2007.
Photograph by Mischa Richter.

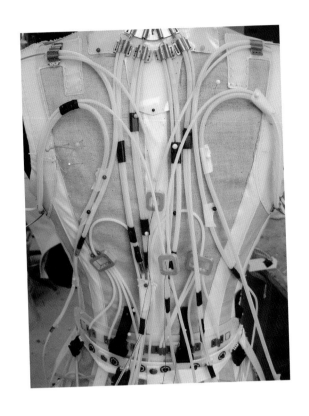

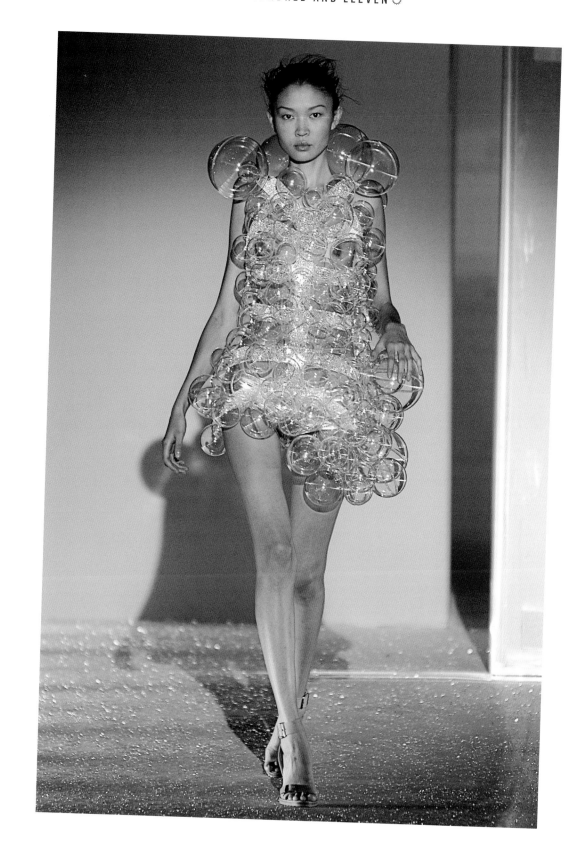

ABOVE:
One Hundred and Eleven, Spring/Summer 2007.
Show photograph by Chris Moore.

OPPOSITE:
V magazine, Spring 2007.
Photograph by Inez van Lamsweerde & Vinoodh Matadin/trunkarchive.com.
Model: Lara Stone.

AIRBORNE
Autumn/Winter 2007
Carreau du Temple, Paris, 28 February 2007, 8.30 p.m.

Presented in four parts: Spring, Summer, Autumn and Winter, *Airborne* commented on how cycles of the weather had parallels with death/life cycles of the body. Chalayan has been constantly interested in the weather as an external power that controls our lives, an inimitable force that is in a constant state of flux. Through the magic of 15,600 LED lamps, combined with crystal displays, the first dress on the catwalk depicted an underwater life form representing summer. High-tech gear was also included, in hats designed to give off a red glow in the dark winter. From protective structures inspired by Japanese samurai armour to fresh blue and white striped dresses paired with shiny rubber leggings, Chalayan explored, in a poetic manner, the resistance to and harmony with nature. *Pamela Golbin.*

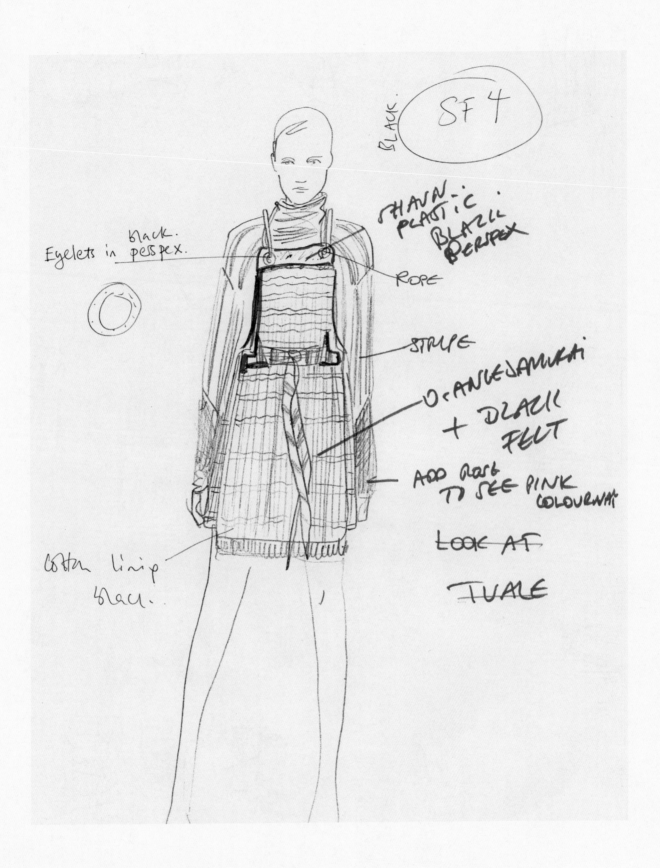

BLACK.

SF 4

SHAUN·IC.
PLASTIC.
BLAZIL
PERSPEX

Eyelets in black.
perspex.

ROPE

STRIPE

O·ANGE·SAMURAI
+ BLAZIL
FELT

ADD ROSE
TO SEE PINK
COLOURWAY

LOOK AT

FUALE

Cotton lining
black.

Airborne, Autumn/Winter 2007.

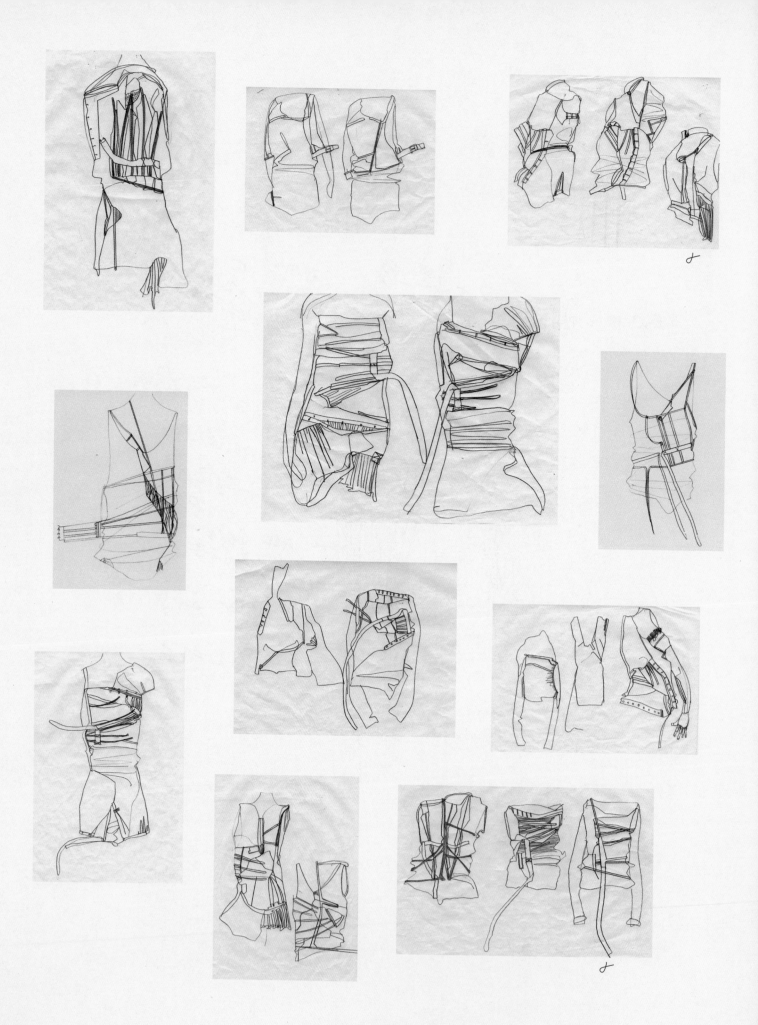

Ambimorphous, Autumn/Winter 2002.

Ambimorphous, Autumn/Winter 2002.

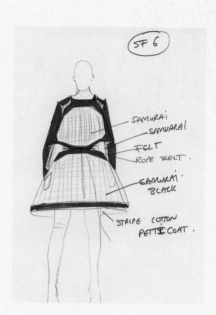

SF 6

SAMURAI
SAMURAI
FELT
ROPE BELT.

SAMURAI
BLACK

STRIPE COTTON
PETTI COAT.

NO 5

SF 7

Samurai

black felt
SHADED AREA
IN FELT

(black lining)

SILK RICH
ROPE FROM
UPHOLSTERS

ORANGE
SAMURAI

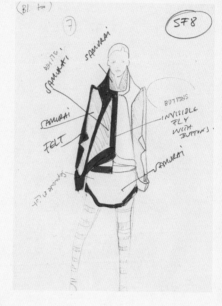

(Bl too)

7

SF 8

WHITE
SAMURAI

SAMURAI

SAMURAI
FELT

BUTTONS
INVISIBLE
FLY WITH
BUTTONS.

SAMURAI

SF 14

b/w
PERSPEX EYELET

BASEBALL
CAP +
PLASTIC CANVAS.

ROPE

FELT
B/W

lined.

SAMURAI
BLACK/WHITE

jersey   or coat?

SF 10

SEAM

BLACK SILK. PIPING
(POSSIBLE)

ORANGE ORGANZA.

SMOKE
ORGANZA.

LINED IN ORANGE?
ORGANZA.

ORANGE → 1m.
SMOKE   1m

SF 15

White
(cotton py)

Bl.
STIFF
NET

SAMURAI FILL COUPE
ORGANZA
(with colour)

red colour

SAMURAI orange
+ ribbon

BLUE OR BLACK
BLUE OR ORANGE

BLACK ORGANZA
(ribbon)

TOGGLES

ORANGE ORNET

FILL
COUPE
ORGANZA
BLACK

DRILL
+ FELT

BLUE / OR ORANGE

BLACK
ORGANZA

ORGANZA
IN BLACK

Still ? collection

accounts at Hussein Chalayan

SF 16

middle

bl.
piping?

SEAM
comes in
slightly

BLUE ORGANZA

tabs + colour SF8

small
little
toggles
twinkler

SAMURAI
ORGANZA.

5

Airborne, Autumn/Winter 2007.

ABOVE AND PREVIOUS PAGES:
Airborne, Autumn/Winter 2007.
Show photographs by Chris Moore.

OPPOSITE:
Hussein Chalayan design notes for a look from *Airborne*,
Autumn/Winter 2007.

SF1. — — —

✳ WHEN CUT, PLEASE **SF1**

PASS SLEEVE FELT TO

~~DRAGAWA~~. ✳ NOT DIRECTLY

TO MACHINIST!

SF **1**	FABRIC DETAILS	CO
THREAD		
FELT (+ FLY)		
SAMURAI		
FELT BACKING COTTON POPLIN		
STRIPE JERSEY		
ROSE TAFFETTA UNDER SLEEVE.		
DUCHESS SATIN.		
ROPES + TAPE AT CENTER F.		
[HOOK + EYE.		
LINING		

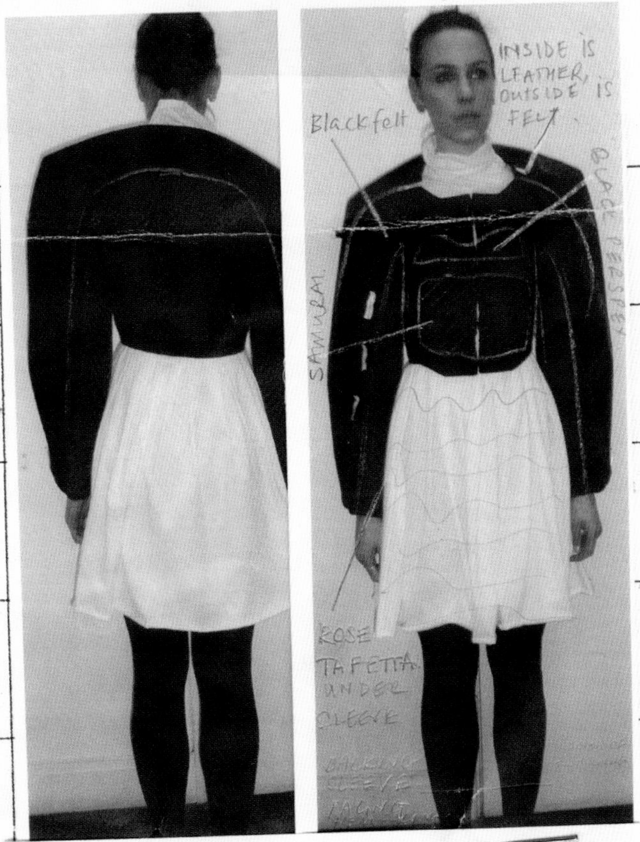

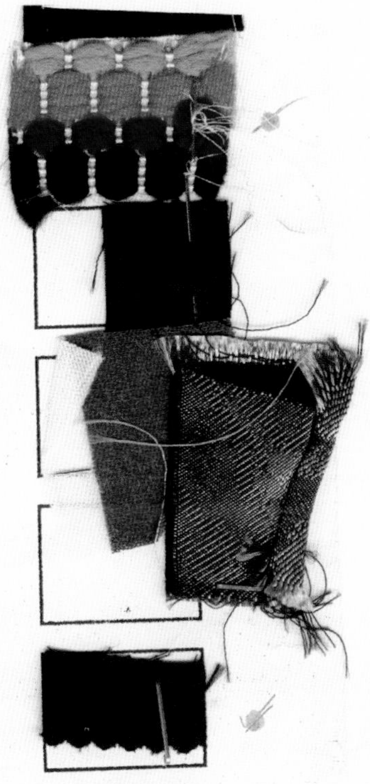

INSIDE IS LEATHER, OUTSIDE IS FELT.

Black felt

SAMURAI

ROSE TAFFETTA UNDER SLEEVE

SF1 ~~FUSING~~.

WE MAY NEED TO FUSE

THE FELT WHERE THE

CRYSTALS ARE (ON SLEEVE)

-PLEASE CHECK WITH

DRAGAWA.

Leather for back inside panel should be fused.

#//AS ITS OWN PATTERN PIECE ✳

OPPOSITE:
Airborne, Autumn/Winter 2007.
Photograph by Chris Moore.

ABOVE:
Airborne, Autumn/Winter 2007.
Show photographs by Chris Moore.

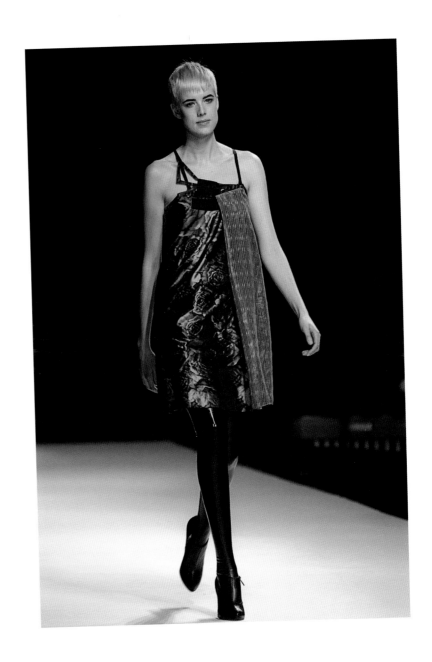

Airborne, Autumn/Winter 2007.
Show photographs by Chris Moore.
Model: Agyness Deyn (above right).

Airborne, Autumn/Winter 2007.
Show photographs by Chris Moore.

TRANSCENDENCE

SPEED AND MOTION

METAMORPHOSIS

BLIND SPOTS

DISEMBODIMENT

NEW ANTHROPOLOGY

MIGRATION

BLIND SPOTS

No art without world. – Alain Robbe-Grillet

A BLIND SPOT is not only what cannot be seen, but it is something that is motivated. There is always a reason for the unseeing due to an obstacle between viewer and *the object* rendering it invisible; or it can be that which exists behind the viewer. In his introduction to the 2008 Oneworld Classics edition of Robbe-Grillet's 1957 novel, *Jealousy*, Tom McCarthy writes: 'In *Jealousy*, [this] blind spot is the novel's protagonist. Through a meticulously – indeed obsessively – described house... moves what film-makers call a... point of view, a camera-and-mic-like node of seeing and hearing. The one thing not seen or heard by this node is the node itself.'

The blind spot, as McCarthy describes it, is the place behind the pen, the camera – or indeed the sewing machine – that ensures that the plot, the narrative has an angle. The real world simply exists, in all its reality; fantasy relies on re-describing, interpreting this reality from a particular point of view. Reality does not cast shadows; narratives cast precise shadows and tell us the time of day. In Alain Resnais's stylish film *Last Year at Marienbad*, for which Robbe-Grillet wrote the original screenplay in 1961, there is a famous scene that takes place in a garden showing a group of people who cast shadows though the trees do not. Man is always motivated, nature is cultivated – clipped, tailored, pruned to man's geometry and scale.

Chalayan's blind spots are fundamental to his constructs – his retelling of the world through its impact on dress, perhaps – a world into which his models walk on as protagonists. We infer his world's abnormalities, by his clothes' preparedness for them, just as we infer Robbe-Grillet's narrator's jealousy by his insistent description, his continual reassembling of the present and the precision of his spatial geometries. Protection is always as choreographed as attack, the chain mail or breastplate and the arrow, or sunglasses and exposure (to the sun or to the spotlight). It is always difficult to tell what comes first: the jealousy or the betrayal.

Chalayan is – very importantly to the development of his work – a filmmaker. In his film *Compassion Fatigue* (2006), Chalayan asks us to perceive man's imposition on the environment and inclusion in it. Chalayan is fascinated by the air re-directed through an air-conditioning unit, water through a fountain and man solidified into a statue, the merging with a physical setting. He is at his most controlled, and perhaps controlling, in his films, his point of view and his attention to detail is palpable – it is in his films that man's triumph is felt (though in Chalayan's hands it is always self aware). Chalayan's preoccupation can be worked out with the camera's ability to lie, to edit, to expose and extrapolate the layering of our experience and to expose our own blind spots.

For Chalayan intellectual references are part of the environment (in *I am Sad Leyla (Üzgünüm Leyla)* (2010), music is open to Persian Poetry or Greek Orthodox chanting, for example). *Heliotropics*, the title of Chalayan's Spring/Summer 2006 collection, is named after the heliotrope, a plant that tracks the sun's motion across the sky – at night the plants have no specific orientation, but at dawn they follow the sun as it rises. This is one of many models of influence and tropism in Chalayan's work. If you want to learn about the sun, you look at what it illuminates, you don't look at it directly. In this sense the sun is a blind spot.
Judith Clark

BLINDSCAPE
Spring/Summer 2005
Couvent des Cordeliers, Paris, 7 October 2004, 5.30 p.m.

Chalayan has noted that '*Blindscape* was originally inspired by how a seeing person with worldly references can try to attempt to see the world from a blind person's viewpoint.' For the designer, the states of sleeping and dreaming are the only moments when the world of the seeing and the blind overlap. Consequently, Chalayan blindfolded himself and sketched the first part of this collection, designing the basics of a wardrobe in a simplified form. Inspired by sleep, shirts, shorts and light summer dresses were made from cottons in blue and white pinstripes. Symbolizing a nightmare, dramatic prints of sea monsters were used as patterns for the third and final grouping. As the ferocious sea died down, sexy blue beaded 'water dresses' emulated the calm and tranquil water after a stormy dream. *Pamela Golbin.*

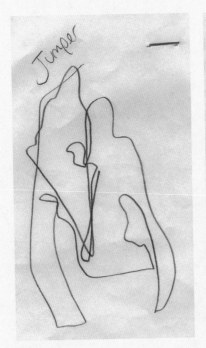

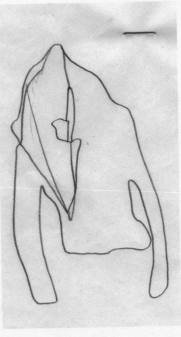

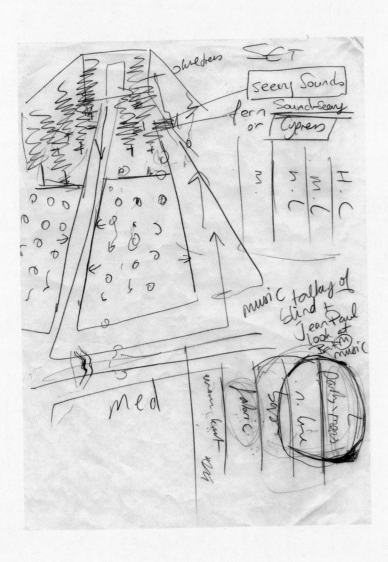

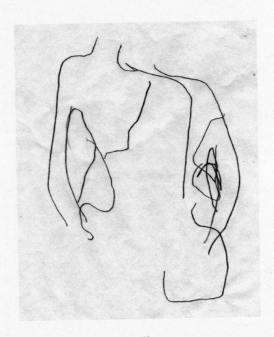

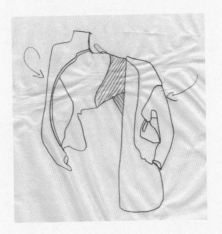

Blindscape, Spring/Summer 2005.
Set drawing (bottom left) and blind-folded sketches.

top   shirt
          lifted up
          with
          braces →
          asymetrical
          tie

↖ take further

jersey trapping
down frilly
skirt part

N BACK FROM
DM CONCIOUS BOARD

↑ overall
with long
strap

↑ see if
you
can take
further

Blindscape, Spring/Summer 2005.

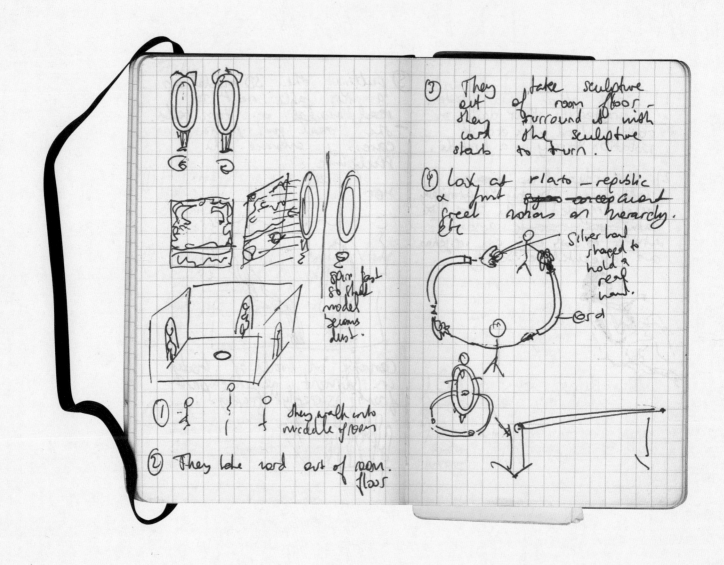

③ They take sculpture
out of room floor —
they surround it with
cord the sculpture
starts to turn.

④ Look at plato — republic
a first ~~egoo~~ consequent
freel actors or hierarchy.
etc

Silver bowl
shaped to
hold a
real
hand.

cord

Spin fast
so that
model
seems
dust.

① they walk into
middle of room

② They take cord out of room.
floor

PAGE 156:
Elle magazine (FR), February 2005.
Photograph by Stéphane Sednaoui.
Model: Gisele Bündchen.

ABOVE LEFT:
Looks from *Blindscape*, Spring/Summer 2005, installed
at Istanbul Modern, 15 July to 24 October 2010.
Photograph by Fatih Metin Demirkol.

ABOVE RIGHT AND THE FOLLOWING PAGES:
Blindscape, Spring/Summer 2005.
Show photographs by Chris Moore.

HELIOTROPICS
Spring/Summer 2006
Carrousel du Louvre, Paris, 6 October 2005, 6.00 p.m.

In his work, Chalayan has explored different archetypical women. At first this archetype was modest and discrete, evolving into a more sexual, desirable and empowered figure. In *Heliotropics*, Chalayan presented short, sexy and body-conscious clothes for his new heroine. By concealing or revealing parts of the body, Chalayan created sculptural silhouettes that accentuated the feminine figure. A biological term, heliotropism refers to the growth of plants, particularly flowers, in response to the stimulus of sunlight. Chalayan established the relation between human beings and nature by exploring a cross-section of aesthetic genres such as art nouveau and rococo that present an ornamental stylization of nature. The dresses in ivory or black and multi-coloured prints trace the female form like beautiful flowers. Reminiscent of blossom stems, piping contours and structures the garments becoming more imposing in the finale dresses to form rope-like elements that delimit boundaries and reference VIP velvet ropes that are used to separate people. *Pamela Golbin.*

Heliotropics, Spring/Summer 2006.
Show photographs by Chris Moore.

OPPOSITE:
Heliotropics, Spring/Summer 2006.
Show photographs by Chris Moore.

ABOVE:
Flair magazine, February 2006.
Photograph by Alexi Lubomirski.
Model: Shannon Click.

FOLLOWING PAGE:
Pop magazine, Spring/Summer 2006.
Photograph by Sølve Sundsbø/Art + Commerce.
Model: Heather Marks.

COMPASSION FATIGUE
A film written and directed by Hussein Chalayan,
premiered at Garanti Galeri, Istanbul, January to March 2006

The four characters in this four-minute film wear clothes from *Heliotropics*, Chalayan's Spring/Summer 2006 collection. The ornate gestures in these garments reference aesthetic genres such as art nouveau and rococo, which Chalayan saw as 'a way of taming nature'. Nature was explored through the ways in which society transforms it. Chalayan showed that these utilitarian interventions have affected the human body and posited spell-casting as an 'alternative form of taming reality'. At the end of the film a spell is cast on the central figure transforming her into a statue.

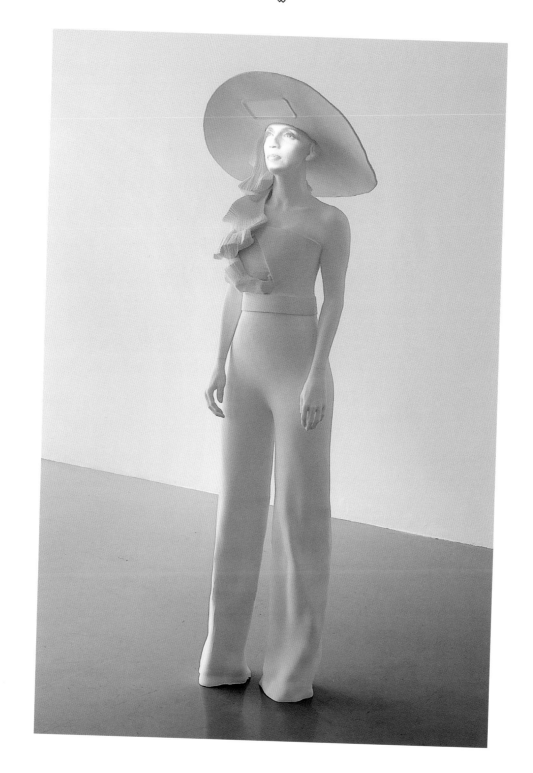

I AM SAD LEYLA (ÜZGÜNÜM LEYLA)
An installation by Hussein Chalayan,
Lisson Gallery, London, 8 September to 2 October 2010

In this gallery environment, Chalayan reframes Turkish classical music –
a genre which has evolved through shifting environments, conquests, political
reforms, geo-political and cultural relations – and introduces a dress code unseen
in Turkish classical performances. This piece of music, so complete in its own
notational and emotional journey, was deconstructed within different zones of
the gallery. One room on the ground floor held only the *voice*, the next exhibited
a life-size sculpture of the *virtuoso* performer Sertab Erener with an image of her
moving face projected onto a life-cast (a development from the projections onto a
three-dimensional printed figure in Chalayan's 2006 film *Compassion Fatigue*).
The main zone in the lower-floor galleries presented the full *performance*, and,
in the final room, the *score* and a projection of the orchestra.

I am Sad Leyla (Üzgünüm Leyla), 2010.
Film still and installation at the Lisson Gallery,
London, featuring Sertab Erener.
Photographs courtesy Lisson Gallery.

ABOVE:
Dazed & Confused magazine, September 1998.
Photograph by Nick Knight.
'Fragmentation' light projections by Hussein Chalayan.
Model: Alison Lapper.

OPPOSITE:
Of Light by Hussein Chalayan, *C* magazine, 2007.
Photographs by Nick Knight.
Projected make-up by Hussein Chalayan.

168

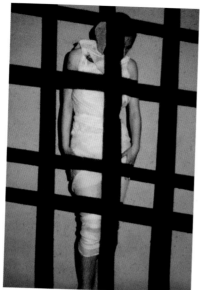

Superimpositions by Hussein Chalayan,
Mid-Warwickshire College, 1988.

TRANSCENDENCE

SPEED AND MOTION

METAMORPHOSIS

BLIND SPOTS

DISEMBODIMENT

NEW ANTHROPOLOGY

MIGRATION

DISEMBODIMENT

IN 1931 Barbara Hepworth made her first 'punctured' form. Henry Moore called 1932 the Year of the Hole. Both of these artists carved voids within helix-shaped bodies of bronze and stone. In his *Manifest Destiny* collection (Spring/Summer 2003), Hussein Chalayan used Lycra – instead of the harder materials favoured by Hepworth and Moore – which, with its tolerance and liberty, resists tailoring in favour of reflecting the body's sinuous lines. These garments employed coiled fabric and layering to mirror the models' musculature and womb centres. Hepworthesque holes pierce the centre of the many of these pieces. Hepworth's iconic void is filled by Chalayan with flesh and blood. Chalayan's sleight of hand suggests Freud's preoccupation with absence and presence and how these ideas might be gendered. Women have been so often portrayed as the hole, the shadow, the negative, to the male positive.

When asked by psychoanalyst Mark Cousins (in the Q&A following Chalayan's lecture about his work to date, at the Architectural Association in London in 2000) whether Chalayan saw any connection in his collections to the body dissected into two, the mother above and the daughter below, Chalayan said 'no – but it is a poetic idea'. *Manifest Destiny* does not escape a reference to the maternal. Curved and amorphous, the designs for the collection are suggestively aligned with nature in contrast to the rigid mathematical grid of graph paper on which other of Chalayan's designs are worked out. This spiral motif seems to continue something begun with the endlessness of the seamless 'looped' dresses in *Panoramic* (Autumn/Winter 1998) and, in doing so, giving them a sort of autonomy from the body, an internal logic and a complex geometry.

Disembodiment seems strange when talking about dress, which is so closely aligned with the body. But when sound, shadow, light/aura are given compositional equivalence, in his catwalk shows, Chalayan is significantly extending the repertoire of the drama of the body and its dress.

It brings our fantasy of what is inside the body onto the outside. Restlessness was visualized when light ricocheted around the models' bodies – sent out from LED rays fixed to their garments – and back onto their figures, bouncing off mirrored surfaces in *Readings* (Spring/Summer 2008). Our identity is projected back at us from our 'audience', all aura and no real body. In this collection the audience became a hypothetically adoring crowd – worshipping at the altar of a celebrity figure. Celebrity is tracked back to ancient sun worship. The body responds prism-like. Chalayan's manner of staging his collections ensures, like shadows, both the isolation of the figure and its emphasis. Chalayan has been preoccupied with celebrity for a long time, needing it to be separate from the word fashion rather than entwined with it; to comment on celebrity is to maintain that distance.

His reference to celebrity has recently become more playful, sexier – the exaggerated sunglasses/hats in *Dolce Far Niente*, (Spring/ Summer 2010), for example, were like a 1960s film set in the Riviera. 'Shadows' under the wide-brim hats of celebrity styling were simulated by translucent black bars covering the model's eyes, with a swath of dark makeup over her face and neck, representing the desire to remain anonymous by flaunting the need to *be* anonymous. Chalayan's distance this time was constructed through his own costume. He was made up, unrecognisable (complete with moustache, toupee, dinner suit and distorted voice) as the show's compère. Chalayan, the author, took on the role of fictional narrator. And in his most recent collection, *Sakoku* (Spring/Summer 2011) (see next chapter, 'New Anthropology'), the whole collection is underlined, underwritten by shadows, and gradually those shadows are given life. The more intense the spotlight, the darker the shadow.

Chalayan believes in the *and* of opposites. Chalayan is questioning the contemporary relevance of Roland Barthes's notion of the aura in a unique work of art and whether that aura can exist within fashion (and now perhaps celebrity culture) and, if so, whether it can be achieved without irony, without the quotation marks. Even the idea of fashion as art now requires quotation marks such is the word's misuse and it is this confusion of categories – the *and* – that Chalayan is interested in.
Judith Clark

LANDS WITHOUT
Spring/Summer 1997
Riverside Studios, London, 28 September 1996, 7.45 p.m.

For *Lands Without*, Chalayan drew his inspiration from women's roles in German fairy tales and their portrayal as scapegoat figures. 'I wanted to look at fairy tales because they portray a certain amount of horror,' Chalayan stated. Literary influences from the novels of British writer Marina Warner and the infamous 15th-century treatise on witchcraft, *Malleus Maleficarum*, served as references in the collection's development. Chalayan's focus in the tale of *Rapunzel* was the character's long blond hair, which connected, for him, to an Aryan sense of empowerment. Chalayan noted: 'I use her hair as kite strings so that [Rapunzel] can escape her tower by flying out.' The title *Lands Without* is taken from Jean-Luc Godard's 1965 film *Alphaville*, whose heroine tries to escape an imposed predicament. *Pamela Golbin.*

ABOVE:
Lands Without, Spring/Summer 1997.
Show photographs by Chris Moore.
Model: Naomi Campbell (above, left).

174

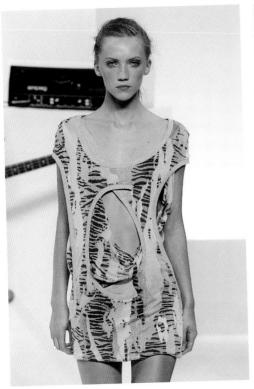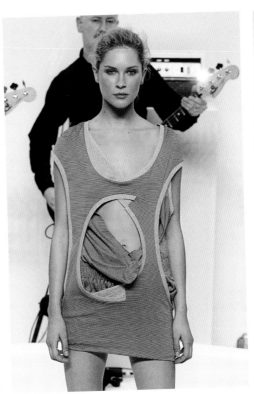

MANIFEST DESTINY

Spring/Summer 2003
Salle Gaveau, Paris, 4 October 2002, 8.00 p.m.

Manifest Destiny refers to the doctrine deployed in the middle of the 19th century
to legitimize America's urge for expansion. Chalayan observed: 'I am interested
in the psychological and the physical implications of imperial expansion, the
way in which this force attempts to civilize our animal state... In *Manifest Destiny*
I wanted to look at the body in its anatomical state and how clothes which cover,
adorn and control could recultivate and reappropriate anatomy, perhaps at times
to an unrecognizable extent disguising all notions of "disgust".' With anatomy as
a starting point, Chalayan explored the meaning of clothes that have been used to
cover, lace-up or deform the body and how these standards can impose Western
ideologies. By using Lycra-infused materials, Chalayan draped the body, liberating
it from constraints through the fabrics' elasticity. He presented a collection of
constructed and deconstructed garments with complex cut-outs and revealing mini-
dresses in abstract prints. The finale dresses offered 'decorative holes' revealing the
abdominal area as if organs had been ripped out leaving nothing but strips of skin.
The music for this show was provided by The Brood, a band directed by musician
Susan Stenger, with choreographer Michael Clark, artist Cerith Wyn Evans and
Chalayan himself performing live on bass guitars. *Pamela Golbin.*

OPPOSITE TOP:
Looks from *Manifest Destiny*, Spring/Summer 2003,
exhibited at Groninger Museum, Groningen, The Netherlands,
17 April to 4 September 2005.
Photograph by Martin de Leeuw.

ABOVE, OPPOSITE BOTTOM AND PAGE 175:
Manifest Destiny, Spring/Summer 2003.
Show photographs by Chris Moore.
Hussein Chalayan and Susan Stenger in background.

ABOVE AND OPPOSITE:
The Face magazine, February 2003.
Photograph by Sølve Sundsbø/Art + Commerce.
Model: Leticia Birkheur.

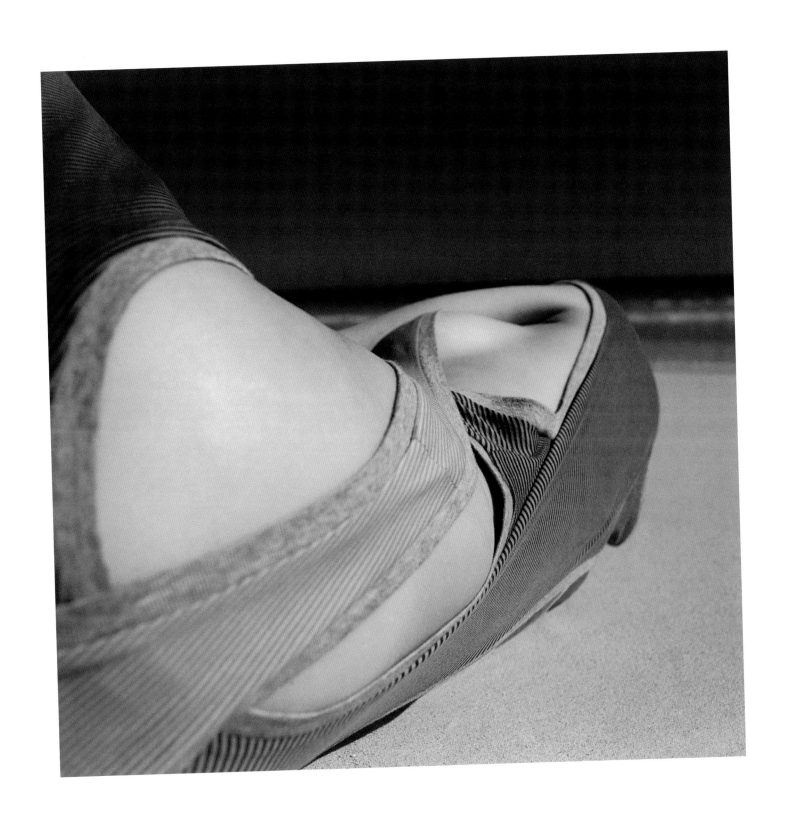

Manifest Destiny, Spring/Summer 2003.
Show photographs by Chris Moore.
Hussein Chalayan, Michael Clark and
Cerith Wyn Evans in background.

180

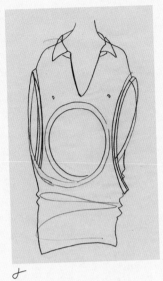

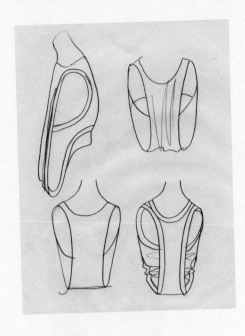

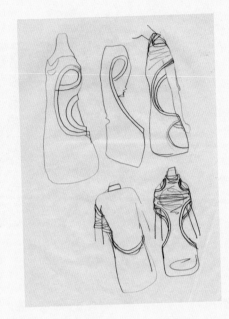

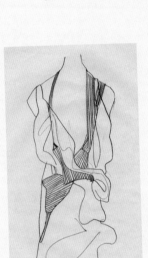

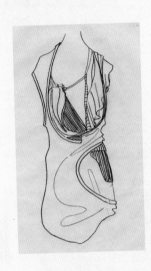

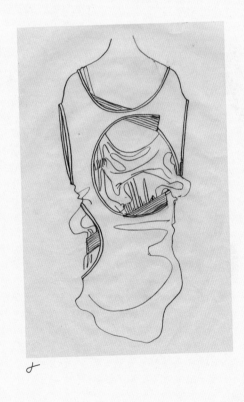

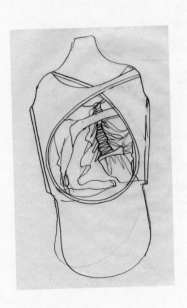

Manifest Destiny, Spring/Summer 2003.

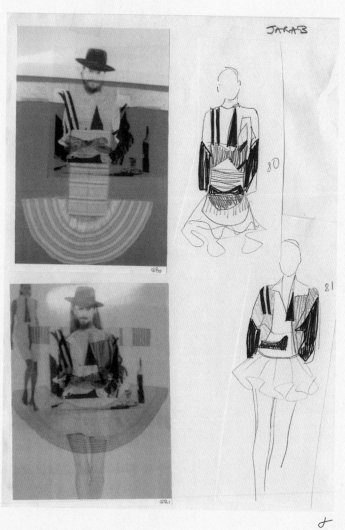

Readings, Spring/Summer 2008.

Readings, Spring/Summer 2008.

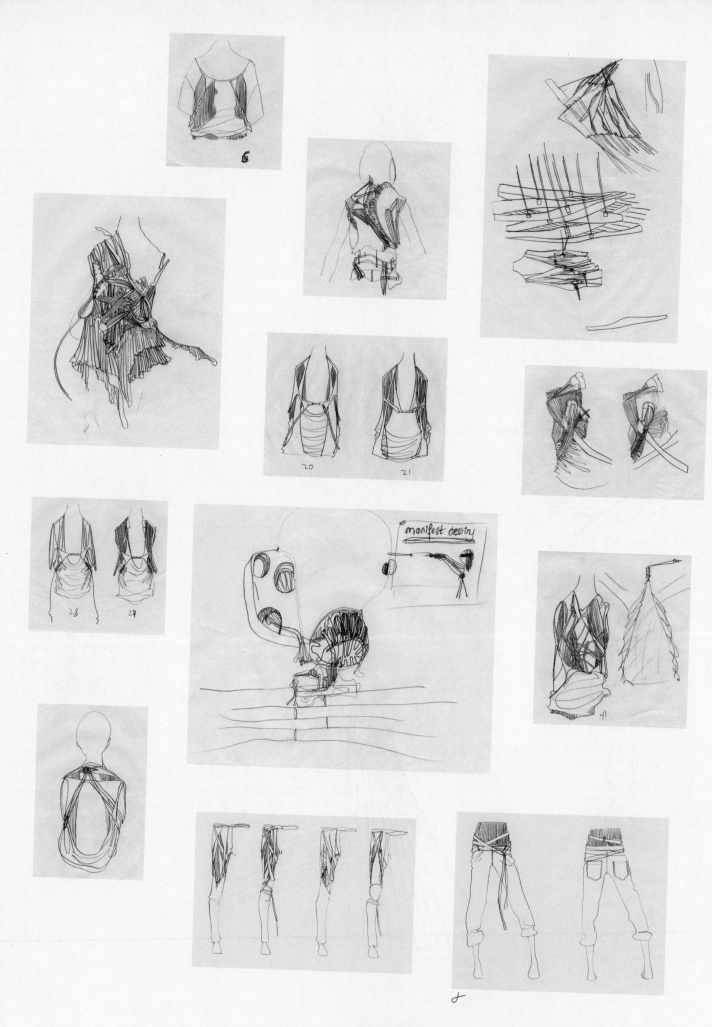

Manifest Destiny, Spring/Summer 2003.

Elle magazine (FR), February 2003.
Photograph by Friedmann Hauss/*Elle*/Scoop.
Model: Audrey Marnay.

ABOVE:
Show invitation for *Manifest Destiny*, Spring/Summer 2003.
Photograph by Marcus Tomlinson.

OPPOSITE:
Readings, Spring/Summer 2008.
Photograph by Moritz Waldemeyer.

READINGS
Spring/Summer 2008
A film by Hussein Chalayan, premiered at Galerie Magda Danysz, Paris,
3 October 2007, 8.00 p.m.

In a film collaboration with Nick Knight's fashion broadcasting company SHOWstudio, Chalayan has once again asserted his commitment to the exploration of technology. Inspired by ancient sun worship and contemporary celebrity status, Chalayan looks at the 'myriad ways different historical, ethnic and religious cultures have worshipped "higher sources" over the centuries'. *Readings* focuses on the cycle of energy between the devotional object and its audience: how icons are made, the rapidity with which they are now accepted into the modern world and how they survive. Hundreds of forms drawn from diverse cultures were morphed and reduced to two composite silhouettes: 'Greek' and 'Jarab' (Jewish/Arab). These composites offered the key stories of the collection along with two sub-themes: Print, arrived at through layering of printed fabrics, and Pois, named after the spotted chiffon from which its dresses are made. The finale showcases, in Chalayan's words, 'the collection's sun-worshipping origins, mapping out an icon's projected and received energy using lasers.' Decorated with Swarovski crystals, the dresses were fitted with 200 moving lasers that gave off high-intensity red beams creating a spectacular light performance. Music was provided by Antony Hegarty of Antony and the Johnsons. *Pamela Golbin.*

Readings, Spring/Summer 2008.
Stills from a video directed by Nick Knight.

OPPOSITE:
Readings, Spring/Summer 2008.
Stills from a video directed by Nick Knight.

ABOVE:
Readings, Spring/Summer 2008.
Photographs by Moritz Waldemeyer.

DOLCE FAR NIENTE
Spring/Summer 2010
Couvent des Cordeliers, Paris, 4 October 2009, 3.00 p.m.

With the air of a 1950s band leader, Chalayan appeared on stage as the master of ceremonies for his *Dolce Far Niente* collection. Wearing a slicked-back, made-to-measure wig, a pencil moustache and sporting an Yves Saint Laurent dark suit, Chalayan narrated in French a description of each of the six distinct design groups that composed the collection: *1950s silhouette crossed with Mongolian technique, evening dress in a minimalist style with a masculine touch, 1950s viewed through the 1990s, towards the beach, dolce far niente on the way to Deauville, Jacobs Ladder.* Progressing through five decades of style, Chalayan gave a modern edge to grown-up glamour. Tailoring with shirting, floor-length dresses in jersey, black leather and white denim, navy blue stripes printed onto organza and white suede were used to create clean, modern and sophisticated silhouettes that sculpted the body. To conjure imagery of the French seaside resort of Deauville, Chalayan used a navy silk plissé with a milk-like fabric to represent ocean waves. In the last section, *Jacobs Ladder*, the garments were punctuated by high-gloss brooches in the form of climbing hands representing, Chalayan said, 'ideas from the historial, religious sense of self-fulfilment – ascension to heaven – juxtaposed with current aspirational bourgeois lifestyle'. *Pamela Golbin.*

Mesdames,
Mesdemoiselles,
Messieurs,
bienvenus au défilé printemps été
deux mille dix d'Hussein Chalayan.

Je suis la cette après-midi pour vous présenter
cette collection qui s'intitule
'dolce far niente'
et qui se divise en 10 groupes

Groupe numéro un:
Silhouette année 50 et références mongoles.
Tailleurs taille-de-guêpe a sequins imprimé
acqua et jersey pour une allure décontractée
— J'aime le côté relax mais couture.

Groupe numéro deux:
Robes du soir sobres et détails masculins.
Longues robes en crêpe de jersey à manches en coton,
remontées façon chemise d'homme.
Découpées un peu trop haut mais j'aime beaucoup.

Groupe numéro trois: les imprimés
Vitraux, images d'utopie et
insertions graphiques sur mousseline.

Groupe numéro quatre:
Les années cinquantes vues à travers
les années quatre-vingt dix.
Tenues en cuir noir et denim blanc.
Rayures tirées vers le bas par une main en trompe l'oeil.
Donnant ainsi sa forme au décolleté.

Groupe numéro cinq: vers la plage…
Les rayures marines courrent sur l'organza
et le daim blanc pour se mélanger
créant ainsi un tissu presque laiteux.

Groupe numéro six: dolce far niente à deauville
Ce groupe incarne un deauville imaginaire.
Le tissu est toujours laiteux,
l'eau est dans les plissés et coule sur la chair.
Chapeau a visiere integrée.

Groupe numéro sept: l'échelle de jacob
Les drapés sont formés par des mains articulées
remontant le long du corps.

OPPOSITE:
Hussein Chalayan preparing for and delivering the French narration
for *Dolce Far Niente*, Spring/Summer 2010.
Photographs courtesy Hussein Chalayan (top) and Chris Moore.

189

Dolce Far Niente, Spring/Summer 2010.
Show photographs by Chris Moore.

OPPOSITE:
Dolce Far Niente, Spring/Summer 2010.
Show photographs by Chris Moore.

ABOVE:
Elle magazine (US), January 2010.
Photograph by Tom Munro. Model: Lady Gaga.

Dolce Far Niente, Spring/Summer 2010.
Show photographs by Chris Moore.

TRANSCENDENCE

SPEED AND MOTION

METAMORPHOSIS

BLIND SPOTS

DISEMBODIMENT

NEW ANTHROPOLOGY

MIGRATION

NEW ANTHROPOLOGY

NEW ANTHROPOLOGY, for Chalayan, is linked to ideas of place and haunted by the notion of the loss of self: the loss (and therefore the possible reconstitution) of the idiosyncrasy of one's heritage. It is about a personal journey during which one makes sure to record something along the way – it might be a road trip, it might be travelling the Silk Route, it might be a single experience, or a nation's DNA. It is about what can be recorded and about wondering what might be lost. What would we know of a person if we were given their precise geographical coordinates?

In Italo Calvino's story *World Memory*, a nameless narrator interviews Müller, the proposed new director of an un-named organization which is creating an archive cataloguing world memory in preparation for the end of human life. Müller has come with excellent credentials for such an undertaking: the project with which he entered the organization is entitled, 'The British Museum in a Nutshell'. Müller and the narrator discuss what is worth preserving at the end of the world:

> *Who could rule out the possibility that the universe consists of the discontinuous network of moments that cannot be recorded, and that our organization does nothing but establish their negative image, a frame around emptiness and meaninglessness.*
>
> ....
>
> *Suppose we received from another planet, a message made up of pure facts, facts of such clarity as to be merely obvious: we wouldn't pay attention, we would hardly even notice; only a message containing something unexpressed, something doubtful and partially indecipherable, would break through the threshold of our consciousness and demand to be received and interpreted.*

What if there ceases to be sharable language? Chalayan is faithful to concepts that do not easily translate into language, or into traceable fact. His motifs, as in *Sakoku* (Spring/Summer 2011), warn us of isolation. The shadows accompanying the 'designed' silhouettes allowing the surface to float free of depth.

In *Panoramic* (Autumn/Winter 1998), the exquisite landscapes from Chalayan's photographic research are abstracted, and are translated into huge pixels of colour as to render the actual place no longer recognisable. Chalayan alludes to roots whilst obscuring them as he goes along. It is as though he is taking away the connections that provide us with our fundamental orientation. Of all his collections, only *Panoramic* carried a quotation (from Ludwig Wittgenstein's *Tractatus*). The quotation has to do with the limits of language and, for Chalayan, about privileging the visual over the verbal: 'What can be said at all can be said clearly, and what we cannot talk about we must pass over in silence.'

Chalayan's *Panoramic* collection was about dress as a territorial claim, what it might be to create a uniform for an unrecognisable ritual, a national dress for a nation that doesn't exist and a costume for an unknown group. The lines of Chalayan's sketches simultaneously create boundaries that define space and shape an identity. But when the walls and floors of the catwalk and stage are mirrored, those same drawn lines are blurred and disorientation is dominant. We are left utterly without coordinates and rely solely on our own reflection to get our bearings. Like the silence created in Goya's Black Paintings, it is a matter, not of narrating history but of seeing it. New identities that cannot be described can nevertheless be clothed, the perspective is always our own. *Judith Clark*

*Italo Calvino, *Numbers in the Dark and Other Stories*, trans. Tim Parks (New York: Pantheon Books 1995), 148-149.

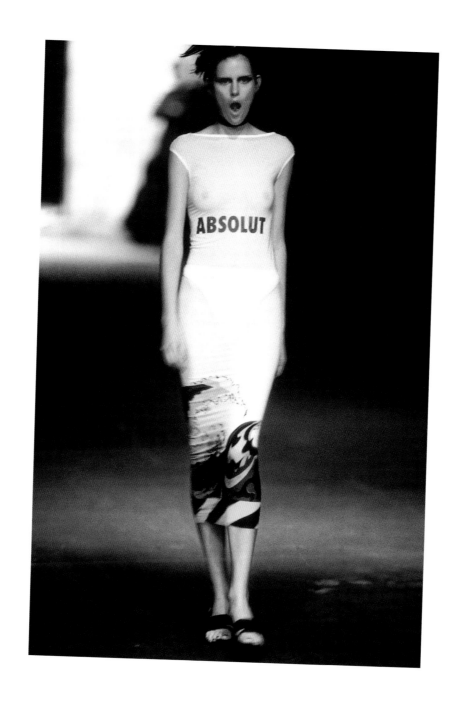

NOTHING, INTERSCOPE
Spring/Summer 1996
Bagleys Warehouse, London, 21 October 1995, 6.00 p.m.

The biblical stories of Noah's Ark and Armageddon inspired Chalayan for this collection. He explained: 'Through narrative, I try to create a look for the body that represents an event.' For *Nothing, Interscope*, Chalayan explored the question: 'If a natural disaster struck the world, how would you react to it?' Originally, the collection was to be shown in a flooded church. Surgical corsets worn over skirts offered an idea of how the body could be reconstructed after a flood or disaster. To create an indelible image that would resist such a catastrophe, Chalayan stated: 'I asked Wakako Kishimoto to paint flowers, which for me, is a universally beautiful thing and it's timeless. We fed her hand-painted patterns to the computer and pixalized them.' Thus preserving her design forever through the digitalization. 'I used Hokusai waves on dresses to represent destruction, the end of the world.' Small sticks to hold the models' lips apart allude to Christian religious paintings depicting the open mouths of bodies ascending to heaven. *Pamela Golbin.*

Nothing Interscope, Spring/Summer 1996.

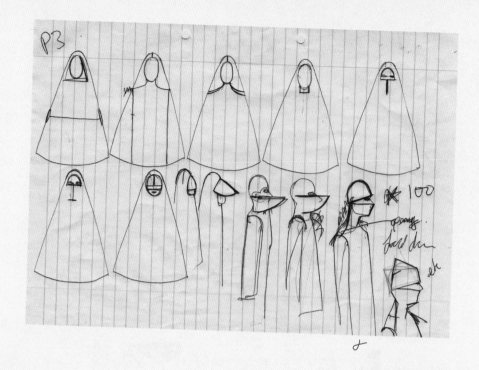

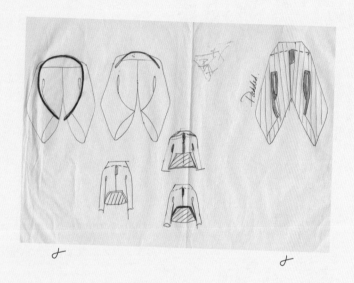

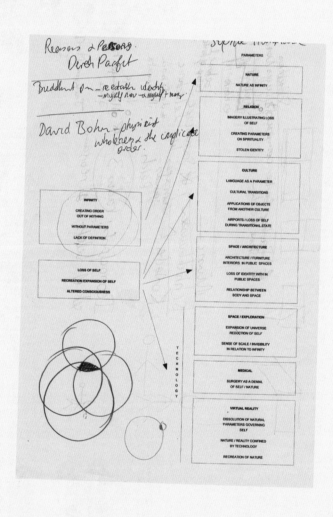

Panoramic, Autumn/Winter 1998.

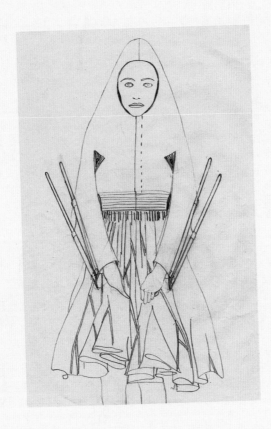

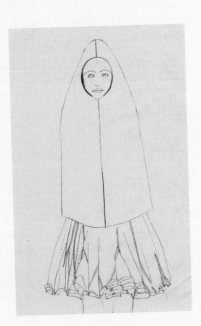

Panoramic, Autumn/Winter 1998.

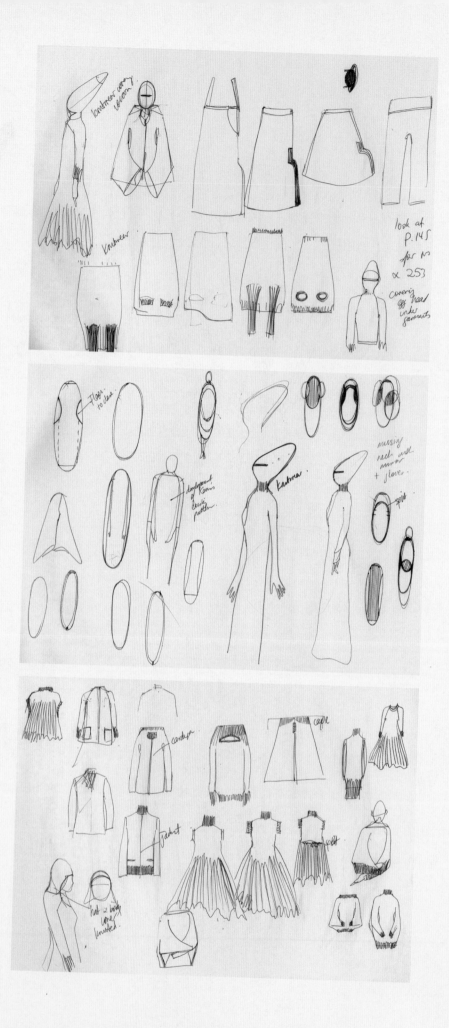

Panoramic, Autumn/Winter 1998.

Nothing, Interscope, Spring/Summer 1996.
Show photographs by Chris Moore.
Model: Stella Tennant (opposite and top right).

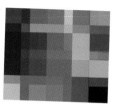

PANORAMIC
Autumn/Winter 1998
Atlantis Gallery, London, 24 February 1998, 8.00 p.m.

With *Panoramic*, Chalayan explored language and its limitations. He explained: 'I looked at the idea of how you define things through language and I wanted to create things that you couldn't describe...' The starting point for the collection was provided by Ludwig Wittgenstein's *Tractatus*, in which the Austrian philosopher argues: 'Whereof we cannot speak, thereof we must be silent.' The limits of language become the limits of thought. Chalayan also expressed that he wanted 'to create a new uniform that couldn't be described,' where the body was lost in parameters that are mostly man-made. Part ethnic costume, part uniform, Chalayan created hybrid garments that camouflaged the individual to blend in with his surroundings resulting in dire anonymity. Mirrors were an important element in the show providing several different and simultaneous views or echoes of reality, exploring both the individual's and the spectator's physical territory as well as their respective roles. Chalayan concluded the show with models holding large coloured building blocks, which were the same colours as the pixellated landscape image projected at the show and that, for Chalayan, symbolized basic elements for constructing everyday reality. *Pamela Golbin.*

OPPOSITE, TOP:
Pixelated landscape images by Chris Levine
for *Panoramic*, Autumn/Winter 1998.

OPPOSITE, BELOW:
Panoramic, Autumn/Winter 1998.
Show photograph by Chris Moore.

ABOVE:
Vogue magazine (UK), July 1998.
Photograph by Nick Knight/*Vogue*/The Condé Nast Publications Ltd.
Model: Daphne Selfe.

ABOVE RIGHT:
Dutch magazine, 1998.
Photograph by Michael Sanders.

THESE AND THE FOLLOWING PAGES:
Panoramic, Autumn/Winter 1998.
Show photographs by Chris Moore.

ABOVE AND OPPOSITE:
Photographs by Richard Avedon.
Carmen Kass and Audrey Marnay, New York, May 1998.
Originally published in *The New Yorker*, 20 July 1998.

Looks from *Panoramic*, Autumn/Winter 1998,
exhibited at the Groninger Museum, Groningen, The Netherlands,
17 April to 4 September 2005.
Photograph by Marten de Leeuw.

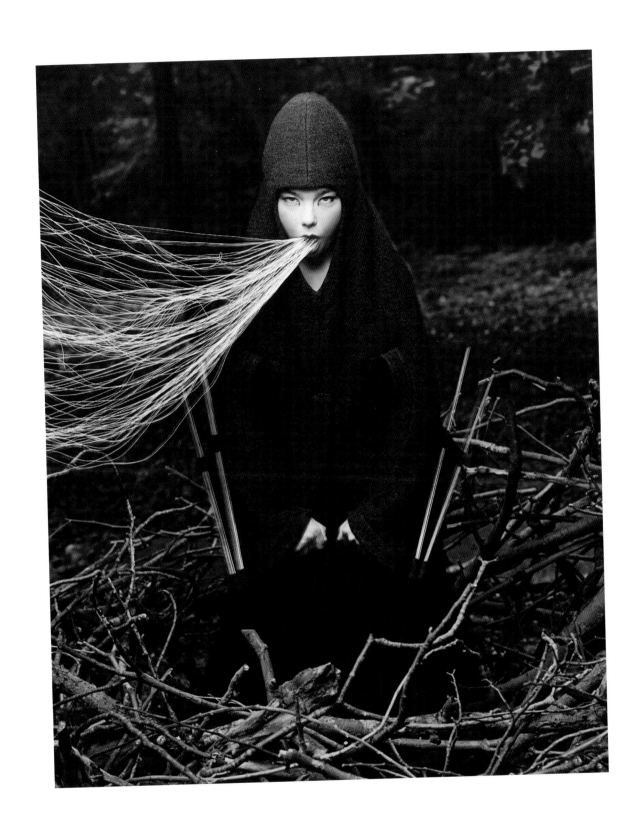

Björk photographed wearing a look from *Panoramic*
for the cover of her 1999 DVD *Volumen*.
Photograph by Inez van Lamsweerde & Vinoodh Matadin/trunkarchive.com.

MAPREADING

Autumn/Winter 2001

Chalayan's *Mapreading* collection opened a new chapter in his design process. Particularly demanding technically, *Mapreading* used 'morphing' techniques to transform each garment in the collection. Like film stills, each silhouette smoothly faded into the next, differing only slightly from the preceding one to recount the mini life-span of a contemporary wardrobe. Beginning with a black coat, all of the classics were accounted for – from the little black dress to the white shirt, the jacket, the denim jacket and finally a version of the 'buried dress'. The decomposed dress crystallized the ravages of time and ended the cycle. But with decay ultimately comes rebirth: the cycle's revival was thus guaranteed. For Chalayan, *Mapreading* was the root of his Spring/Summer 2007 collection, *One Hundred and Eleven*, in which five hand-constructed, mechanically engineered dresses morph from one era to another. *Pamela Golbin.*

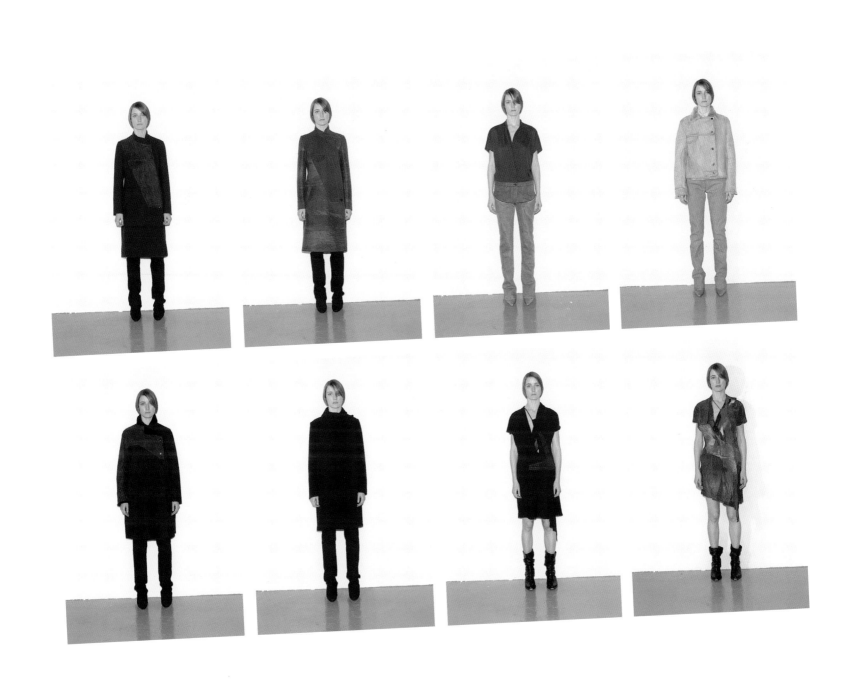

Mapreading, Autumn/Winter 2001.
Photographs by Marcus Tomlinson.

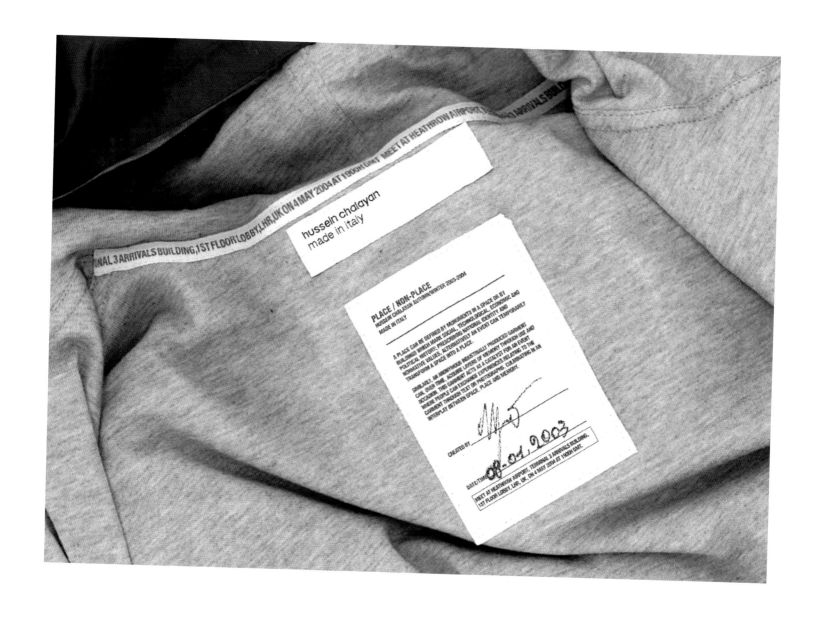

PLACE/NON-PLACE
Menswear, Autumn/Winter 2003
Event at Heathrow Airport, London, 4 May 2004

Place/Non-Place was an interactive event coinciding with Chalayan's Autumn/Winter 2003 menswear collection of the same name. Inspired by French anthropologist Marc Augé's description of airports as 'non-places', Chalayan became interested in the idea of temporarily turning a non-place into a 'place' through an event instigated by clothes. Chalayan attached labels inside his garments, inviting buyers to gather at Heathrow about 10 months after the collection was available. After 10 months, one person turned up at Heathrow and met with two members of Chalayan's design team, who took photos and interviewed this individual. Chalayan described his intention: 'Many garments containing pockets for specially collected objects could have been bought along to the event, where strangers could have created a dialogue through the significance of these objects for them or by simply sharing their reasons for buying the clothes etc, ultimately garments becoming a token for communication whilst also turning the non-place into a temporary place.' *Pamela Golbin.*

HUSSEIN CHALAYAN, THE MEETING POINT GERT JONKERS

Hussein Chalayan ne se contente pas de créer une nou-velle ligne pour hommes. Il met en scène le futur de cette ligne, son après show-room et prédit un instant de vie aux heureux possesseurs de ses t-shirts : *Rendez-vous au Lobby du 1er étage du bâtiment des Arrivées Terminal 3 de l'aéroport d'Heathrow-Londres le 4 mai 2004 à 19H00*. C'est écrit sur le t-shirt. RDV le 4 mai pour connaître ceux qui prennent Chalayan au pied de la lettre.

Hussein Chalayan hasn't stopped at merely creating a new line for men. He offers his line of clothing in his après show-room and he foresees a moment in the life of the happy few who own his t-shirts: *Rendez-vous at Heathrow-London Airport 1st Floor Lobby, Arrival Building, Terminal 3 on the 4th of May 2004, 19:00 GMT*. It's written on the t-shirt. Let's meet there on that date and see who took Chalayan at his word.

–'Heathrow Press Office, this is Matt speaking. How can I help you?'
–Hello Matt, this is Gert Jonkers calling on behalf of the French maga-zine Le colette. I'm writing an article on this fashion designer Hussein Chalayan, whose new men's wear collection is kind of built around the idea of a possible get-together at Heathrow airport on Tuesday, the 4th of May next year. He is asking people to come to the 1st Floor Lobby in the Terminal 3 Arrivals Building on May 4, 2004, at 7 pm, GMT. Have you heard of it?
–'No, we've not been alerted to that. You're saying it's May 4th next year?'
–Yeah.
–'Okay. And he's holding a press conference or something?'
–I don't know. It's more like, some of the T-shirts in the collection have this print saying 'Let's meet at this lobby at Heathrow airport on May 4th', blah-blah-blah. My question to you is whether the place he mentions is actually accessible to everybody.
–'I'm not sure on that, actually. So what he's saying is…or let's start from the beginning: you're calling from which magazine?'
–It's a magazine called Le colette.
–'Le colette.'
–Right. It's affiliated with this department store colette in Paris.
–'Okay. And you're calling from Amsterdam?'
–Yeah.
–'And who's the French designer

then?'
–No no no, he's from London. His name is Hussein Chalayan. I think he's Turkish-Cypriot, but he lives in London.
–'And how do we spell his surname?'
–C-h-a-l-a-y-a-n.
–'All right. And so his idea is… He's selling what?'
–He made a men's wear collection for autumn-winter 2003-2004 and it's all based on travelwear. The collars of the shirts may have room to expand just like travelbags can expand, like a little harmonica, and there are T-shirts that come in an airmail envelope, and there's that text mentioning the meeting on May 4, 2004, and… I'm not saying he literally expects people to meet him that day, I guess for him the meeting is more a way of pinpointing the idea of travelling to an actual place and time.
–'Hmm. And, let me see, all those people that come on May the 4th will actually be travelling, you believe?'
–Well, I don't know. That's actually my question for you: Can one get to that specific lobby without an air ticket? Would you need to go through customs first to get there?
–'Well, the thing is, we'll need to look into that. Luckily it's a long way off; there's still more than a year to go, right? We'll probably need to have a chat with the guy himself, too. I've not heard of any requests to hold, you know, an event like this here.'

–That's what I was just saying: I don't think Hussein will actually be doing anything special there. The idea of the meeting at Heathrow may all just be in his dreams.
–'Well, yeah, but still, we'll need to look into this. Let me take your number and I'll find it out for you.'
–Would you have time to look into it today?
–'It'll probably be in the next few days, 'cause we'll need to dig around and find out what's going on there. Luckily it's a long way off. We're talking about May next year, right?'
–Yes, but our deadline is a bit closer than that, you see?
–'Oh, so you're actually writing an article on this?'
–Yeah. And, like I said, therefore I was just curious about whether or not that place is accessible for everybody, or only for the lucky few air travellers, or only for business-class travellers, or…
–'That's why we'll probably need to have a chat with him first. Or at least find out if somebody has already had a chat with him. I would say everybody coming through the lobby would have to be either travelling or meeting somebody who's travelling.'
–Would you happen to know what sort of place it is that he mentions? Is there an actual lobby on the 1st floor of the Terminal 3 Arrivals Building or did Hussein make it all up?
–'That I'd have to find out too. I must say I have no clue.'

25

Text by Gert Jonkers for *Place/Non-Place*, May 2004, published by Colette, Paris.

Polaroid photographs of Peter Orlov, the only participant
in the Heathrow Airport event on 4 May 2004 for
Place/Non-Place, menswear, Autumn/Winter 2003.
Photographs courtesy Hussein Chalayan.

hussein chalayan

place / non-place
autum / winter 2003-2004

A PLACE CAN BE DEFINED BY MONUMENTS IN A SPACE OR BY BUILDINGS WHICH MARK SOCIAL, TECHNOLOGICAL, ECONOMIC AND POLITICAL HISTORY, PRESCRIBING NATIONAL IDENTITY AND NORMATIVE VALUES. ALTERNATIVELY AN EVENT CAN TEMPORARILY TRANSFORM A SPACE INTO A PLACE.
SIMILARLY, AN ANONYMOUS INDUSTRIALLY PRODUCED GARMENT CAN, OVER TIME, AQUIRE LAYERS OF MEMORY THROUGH USE AND OCCASION. THIS GARMENT ACTS AS A CATALYST FOR AN EVENT WHERE PEOPLE CAN EXCHANGE EXPERIENCES RELATING TO THE GARMENT THROUGH TEXT OR PHOTOGRAPHS, CULMINATING IN AN INTERPLAY BETWEEN SPACE, PLACE AND MEMORY.

MEET AT HEATHROW AIRPORT, TERMINAL 3, ARRIVALS BUILDING, 1ST FLOOR LOBBY, LHR, UK, ON 4 MAY 2004 AT 1900 GMT.

QUESTIONNAIRE FOR PLACE / NON-PLACE EVENT PARTICIPANTS

1. WHAT DID YOU THINK WHEN YOU FIRST READ THE TEXT ABOVE? I was intrigued by the idea - having known about Hussein's work from the past, I wanted to see how the menswear would turn out - and suspected that the strongly conceptual element in his work would have to be

2. WHAT MADE YOU PARTICIPATE THIS EVENT? Curiosity - what would the event involve? Who are the other people who are interested in / buy Hussein's clothing (or other conceptual design)? Ultimately, the worst that would have happened is I would have wasted an hour of my life - not that huge a loss.

3. IS THERE SOMETHING YOU WOULD LIKE TO SHARE WITH US? The pockets in the jacket are really useful. It's well designed - thanks. Nothing else, I guess - or nothing that isn't too tangential... out-weighed by the potential benefits

4. WHAT IS THE MOST IMPORTANT MEMORY YOU HAVE HAD WHILE WEARING THIS GARMENT? Difficult to say - seeing my ex-boyfriend for the first time after splitting up, a good night out clubbing, books I've read. It's hard to rate these in any way and I guess it would be a bit pointless to try...

5. CAN WE HAVE THE PERMISSION TO USE YOUR PHOTO AND THIS QUESTIONNAIRE FOR A FUTURE EXIBITION?

✓	YES		NO

6. PERSONAL DETAILS*

NAME: Peter Orlov

TEL:

E-MAIL:

*OPTIONAL, IF YOU WOULD LIKE TO BE INVITED TO FUTURE EVENTS.

HCpnpAW03-100

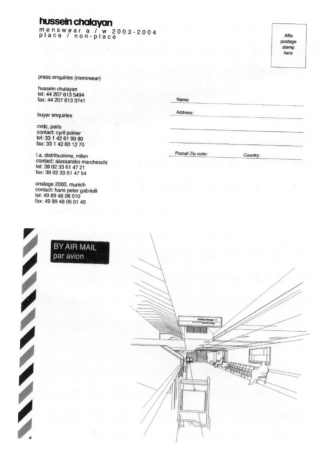

hussein chalayan
menswear a / w 2003-2004
place / non-place

Affix
postage
stamp
here

press enquiries (menswear)

hussein chalayan
tel: 44 207 613 5494
fax: 44 207 613 3741

buyer enquiries

cvdc, paris
contact: cyril poirier
tel: 33 1 42 61 99 80
fax: 33 1 42 60 12 70

l.a. distribuzione, milan
contact: alessandro marcheschi
tel: 39 02 33 61 47 21
fax: 39 02 33 61 47 54

onstage 2000, munich
contact: hans peter gabrielli
tel: 49 89 48 06 010
fax: 49 99 48 06 01 40

Name:

Address:

Postal/ Zip code: Country:

BY AIR MAIL
par avion

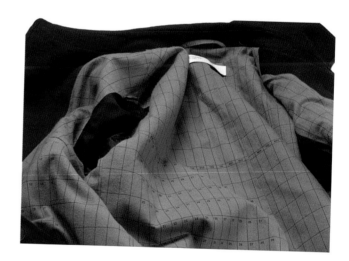

Invitation and looks for
Place/Non-Place, Autumn/Winter 2003.

  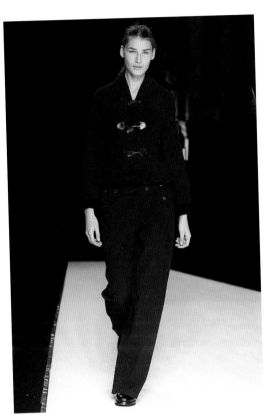

ANTHROPOLOGY OF SOLITUDE
Autumn/Winter 2004
Le Grand Hôtel, Paris, 5 March 2004, 12.30 p.m.

For *Anthropology of Solitude*, Chalayan was interested in the definition of the 'self' not only the initial sense of personal identity as formed during childhood but also the 'national self' and the contemporary 'isolated self'. He elaborated: 'In our technologically driven society, speed and communication have become paradigms underwriting our thoughts, actions and how we perceive ourselves. Consequently, this is creating a new anthropology of the isolated and autonomous individual.' Black coats in fake fur were hooded to represent capsules for solitude. Garments with CD pockets emphasized self-containment sealing off the wearer from the outside world. To convey a nationalistic feeling, prints and jacquards depicted Turkish historical images from the creation of the Republic in 1923 up through the 1950s. *Pamela Golbin.*

Anthropology of Solitude, Autumn/Winter 2004.
Show photographs by Chris Moore.

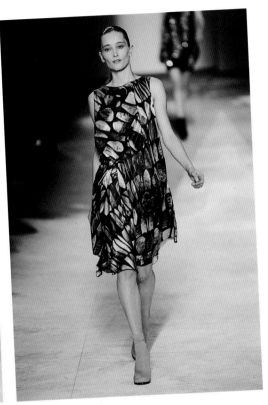

GRAINS AND STEEL

Autumn/Winter 2008
Musée de l'Homme, Paris, 27 February 2008, 8.00 p.m.

In *Grains and Steel*, Chalayan explored the evolution of humanity and its transformation from the Stone Age to the Steel era. A five-person a cappella group set the tone, producing an extraordinary array of abstract and realistic sounds – from outer space, a jungle folkloric and religious vocals. Soft black dresses, asymmetrical, draped and with printed stone patterns hinted at Chalayan's interest in life sciences, where human behaviour and cultural codes are brought together through anthropological stories of space and technology. Like explorers from another age, the two models of the finale came out from the dark dressed in tight black one-piece suits with protruding light elements that were to guide them through the Big Bang of the universe. *Pamela Golbin.*

ABOVE:
Grains and Steel, Autumn/Winter 2008.
Backstage photograph by Claire Robertson.

OPPOSITE:
Grains and Steel, Autumn/Winter 2008.
Show photographs by Chris Moore.

Grains and Steel, Autumn/Winter 2008.
Show photograph by Chris Moore.

Grains and Steel, Autumn/Winter 2008.

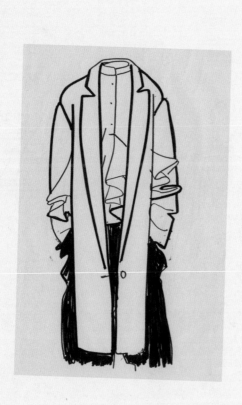

Sakoku, Spring/Summer 2011.

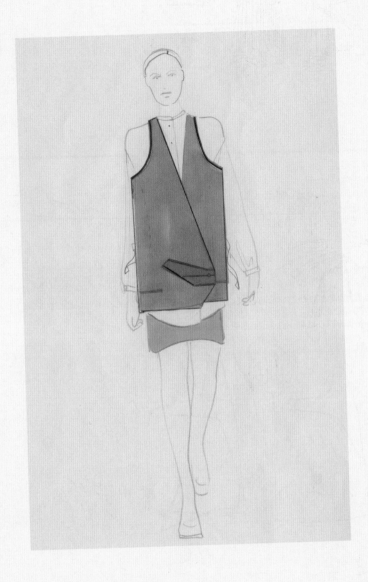

Sakoku, Spring/Summer 2011.

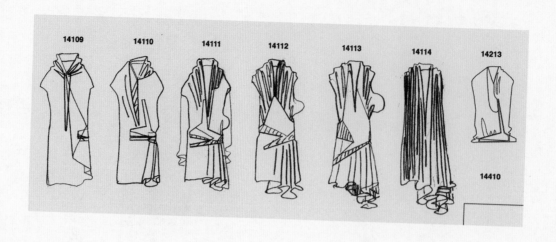

Mapreading, Autumn/Winter 2001.

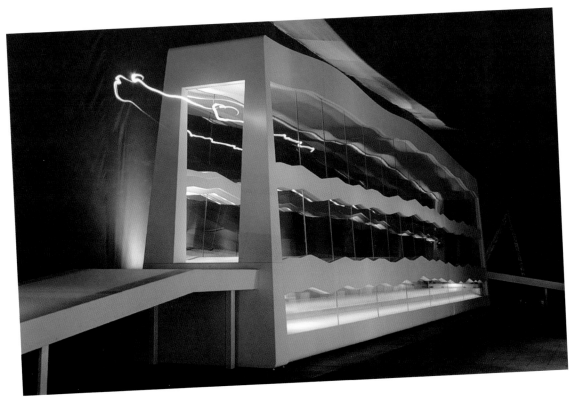

THE TUNNEL
2008
Center for Architecture and Design, Mexico City

This project was commissioned by Level Vodka, as a desire to create an installation that would introduce the drink to new markets. *The Level Tunnel* (15 metres long and five metres high) was made of fibreglass, glass and leather. Scent, sound and touch were combined to create an interactive space leading to a new 'sense'. Inside the tunnel, visitors were blindfolded but able to hear and control, through their movements, pre-recorded music played on a flute made from a Level Vodka bottle itself. Walking through a breeze of ingredients of the drink such as citrus and cedar (released at different zones as the individual passed through), visitors were able to sense a merging of different elements of the drink as a 'spacial' synaesthetic experience. Photographs courtesy Absolute Vodka.

sakoku

wrapping in transition

haiku

imminence of water

decentred

shadow readings

floating body

SAKOKU

Spring/Summer 2011
Galerie Deborah Zafman, Paris, 1 to 7 October 2010

For this collection, Chalayan did not present a fashion show but instead produced a film which he directed. Entitled *Sakoku* or 'locked country', the title is the name of Japan's foreign relations policy of isolation, which, until the mid-19th century, banned almost all foreigners from entering the country and any Japanese from leaving under penalty of death. Chalayan explored how shadow, water, architecture, technology, theatre, costume, poetry and isolation all affect Japanese culture. He said: 'Japan is saturated with disembodied experiences in a decentered space where event is born out of the choreography of ceremony and the simulation of thought.' In six themes, Chalayan presented an abstract take on Japan: *decentered, wrapping in transition, shadow reading, imminence of water, haiku* and *floating body*. Chalayan used wide panels of *broderie anglaise* to enclose the body like a gift waiting to be opened. Mesh fabrics recalled the wicker sliding doors used to divide Japanese interior spaces. Jade green, fuchsia pink, earthy olive, mustard and light beige are applied in blocks following the colour tradition of kabuki. *Pamela Golbin.*

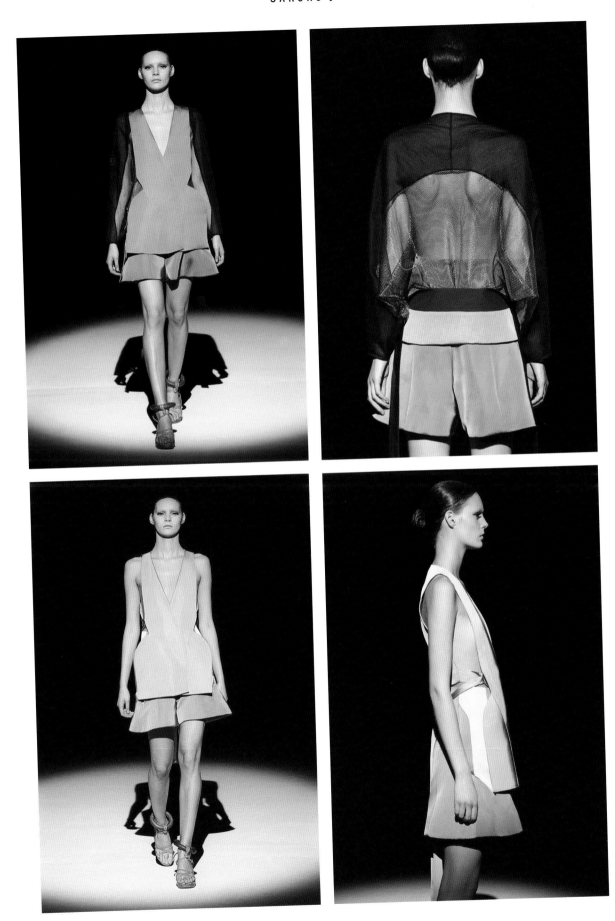

Sakoku, Spring/Summer 2011.
Stills from a video by Hussein Chalayan.

THESE AND THE FOLLOWING PAGES:
Sakoku, Spring/Summer 2011.
Stills from a video by Hussein Chalayan.

存

在

す

る

ABOVE LEFT AND TOP:
The *Haiku Dress* from *Sakoku*, Spring/Summer 2011.
Stills from a video by Hussein Chalayan.

ABOVE RIGHT:
Son of Sonzai Suru, 2010.
An installation by Hussein Chalayan for the exhibition
GSK Contemporary - Aware: Art Fashion Identity,
Royal Academy of Arts, London, 2 December 2010 to 30 January 2011.
Commission by the Royal Academy of Arts and London College of Fashion.
Photograph © Royal Academy of Arts, London/Andy Stagg.

TRANSCENDENCE

SPEED AND MOTION

METAMORPHOSIS

BLIND SPOTS

DISEMBODIMENT

NEW ANTHROPOLOGY

MIGRATION

MIGRATION

...every point of thought is the centre of an intellectual world – the two uppermost thoughts in a Man's mind are the two poles of his World he revolves on them and every thing is southward or northward to him through their means. – John Keats, from a letter to Benjamin Bailey

PROFESSOR JOHN PICKLES begins his wonderful book *A History of Spaces: Cartographic reason, mapping and the geo-coded world** with a quote from *Cartographies*, a 1989 collection of short stories by Maya Sonenberg[†]: 'It has always been this way with the map-makers: from their first scratches on the cave wall to show the migration patterns of the herds, they have traced lines and lived inside them.' Pickles acknowledges, as does Chalayan, that the drawing of a line is, first of all, a fundamental geographical and spatial act, in which 'the geographical imagination is pushed to what [the Swedish geographer, Gunnar Olsson] called the "dematerialized point of abstractness"'.

For *Between* (Spring/Summer 1998), Chalayan gave nude models lengths of rope and pegs with which to fix these lengths into the sand on a beach. By doing so the models created a territory. This performance emphasized how fundamental this act of claiming land is, and also that we can carry land with us, and within us: that this act could be performed anywhere. The beach where the performance took place, in Dungeness on the shores of East Sussex, had very few identifying features – but what we do know is that, in England, beaches are public property.

It is from this place that we perceive the rest of the world; from there that we migrate North – the more harsh and remote places in our imagination – or to the milder sunnier South. Perhaps we move between London and Istanbul. We travel into and away from the sun in our minds – winter and summer. We can fly to another season – something we still feel to be a magical gesture of escape. If you look carefully at Chalayan's early drawings, you will find some have been rendered on the headed paper of the London Travel Centre.

Escape is the word most associated with Chalayan's version of travel, imaginative escape and escape from persecution. The recording of the accumulation of travelled paths is like a new kind of portrait. Engines rev up in anticipation of a trip across five states of America: city hoods to coy yet puritanical straw bonnets in one collection reflecting the country's incongruity and vastness. Clothes reflect the roads taken. An incremental integration into a different society – from national dress to little black dress within one collection. Clothes contain a world on the move.

Afterwords, Chalayan's landmark collection from Autumn/Winter 2000, is described by the designer as 'creating the means in which to carry possessions away more easily at the time of attack'. The pocket of one garment was fused with a handbag, another coat pocket had been tailored into the shape of an umbrella. Most famously, the upholstery covering four chairs was converted by models into dresses, after which the chairs' supporting structures were collapsed and re-formed into suitcases in a matter of choreographed seconds. Then the finale – a model stepped into the centre of a circular table, pulled it up around her waist and hitched it to her belt. As she smoothed the table down her hips and legs, it was transformed into multi-slatted wooden skirt. *Les Voix Bulgares* choir sang behind a gauze screen creating a strange, meditative plea, prayer or lament – the nature ofthe song was, importantly, never clear, it was important just that the sound came from elsewhere. As always, Chalayan's references to time and place were not specific. He could have been referring to any marginalised group, on any minimalist stage, in an interior that might have been anywhere. Suggesting that persecution could happen to anyone. *Judith Clark*

*John Pickles, *A History of Spaces: Cartographic reason, mapping and the geo-coded world* (Routledge: London, 2003).
†Maya Sonenberg, *Cartographies* (Ecco: New York, 1989).

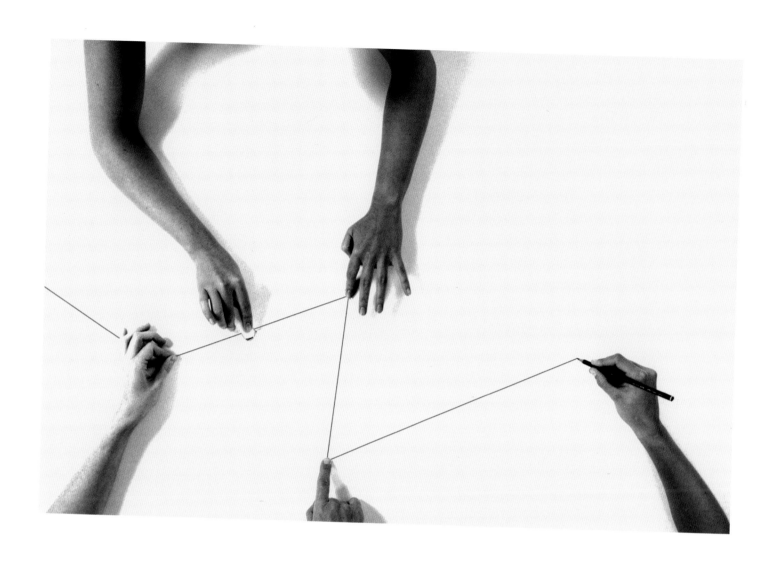

GEOTROPICS

Spring/Summer 1999
Atlantis Gallery, London, 28 September 1998, 8.30 p.m.

A biological term, *geotropics* refers to the oriented growth of an organism with respect to the force of gravity. Integrating the notion of nature and its forces, Chalayan's collection *Geotropics* reflected upon the role of natural topographical features, such as mountains and rivers, as well as human actions, such as wars, in shaping the definition of a nation. Chalayan used the body to create a micro-geography. In a computer-animated film, he brought together national costumes from different places and eras along the 2000-year-old Silk Route which extends from China to the West. The film was a journey through time and space, morphing garments from one to another. Two monumental dresses were presented in the finale. In one, head and armrests constituted a chair that was integrated into the model's clothing forming the silhouette and its wearer into a single and unique entity. *Pamela Golbin.*

Geotropics, Spring/Summer 1999.

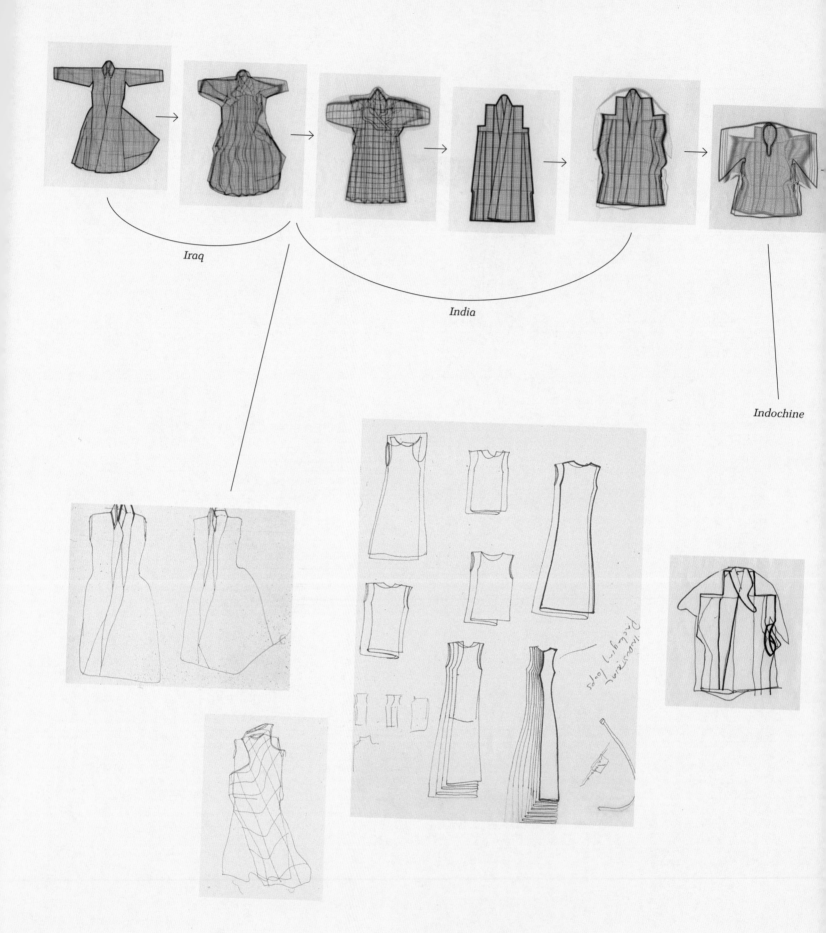

Iraq

India

Indochine

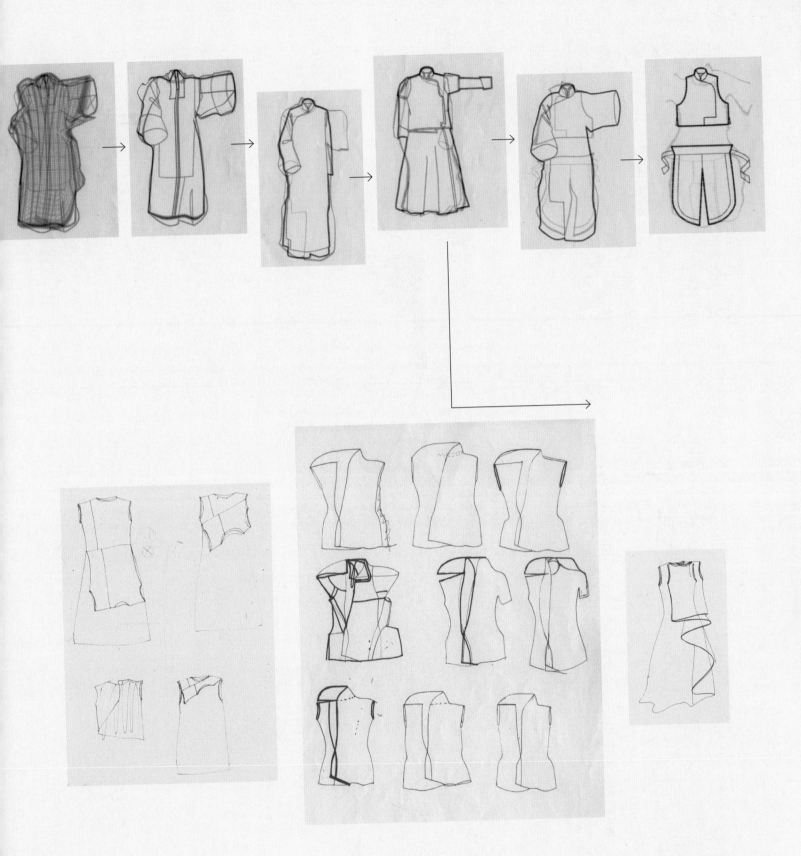

Geotropics, Spring/Summer 1999.

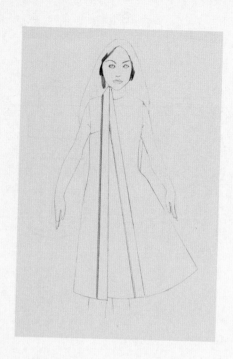
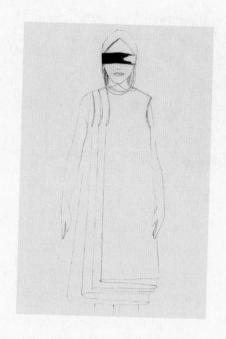
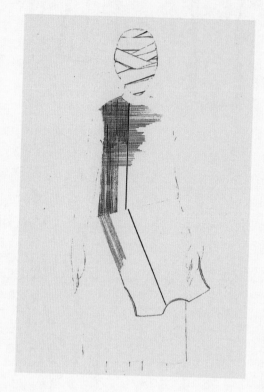

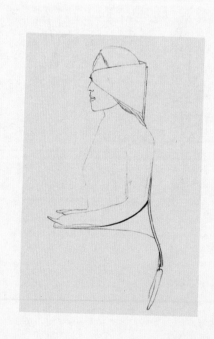

Geotropics, Spring/Summer 1999.

PAGE 234:
Show invitation for *Geotropics*, Spring/Summer 1999.
Photograph courtesy Hussein Chayalan,
graphics by Chris Levine.

ABOVE:
Geotropics, Spring/Summer 1999.
Photographs by Marcus Tomlinson.

Geotropics, Spring/Summer 1999.
Show photographs by Chris Moore.

Geotropics, Spring/Summer 1999.
Show photographs by Chris Moore.

AFTERWORDS
Autumn/Winter 2000
Sadler's Wells Theatre, London, 16 February 2000, 8.30 p.m.

Inspired by the plight of the refugee and the horror of being displaced in times of war, *Afterwords* makes reference to how Turkish Cypriots were subjected to ethnic cleansing in Cyprus prior to the division of the island in 1974. Chalayan revealed: 'This project started off from the war in Kosovo and then I connected it to what happened in Cyprus which was quite similar, when Greek EOKA sympathizers, in an attempt to unite Cyprus to Greece, were terrorizing Turkish Cypriot homes.' In this collection, Chalayan explored the reactions of people who are confronted by war and their need to hide their possessions or to carry them on their exodus. Chalayan staged his collection in a minimal white space that was set up like a living room, with four sitting room chairs, a table, a flat-screen television and an object-filled shelf. First, an average family walked on stage: mother, father, grandmother and children. Then from a hidden door, models appeared in seemingly simple clothes and began to seize, one by one, the objects in the room, fitting them into special pockets in their garments designed to contain them. Finally, models wearing simple grey shift dresses entered, removed the chair covers and proceeded to put them on. One last model, stepped inside the wooden table and pulled it up her legs and waist, transforming it into a voluminous skirt. The chairs were folded up to become suitcases and the models exited the set. The white room was left completely empty and lifeless. *Pamela Golbin*.

OPPOSITE:
Don McCullin, portrait of a grieving Turkish Cypriot woman,
Ghaziveram, Cyprus, April 1964.
Photograph courtesy Don McCullin.

ABOVE:
Afterwords, Autumn/Winter 2000.
Show photographs by Chris Moore.

Afterwords, Autumn/Winter 2000.
Show photographs by Chris Moore.

Afterwords, Autumn/Winter 2000.
Show photographs by Chris Moore.

Afterwords, Autumn/Winter 2000.
Show photographs by Chris Moore.

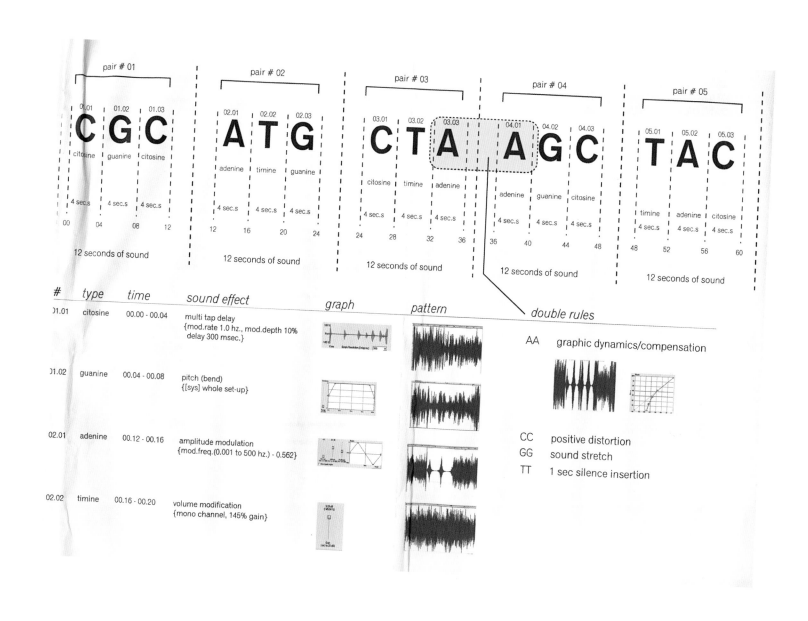

GENOMETRICS

Autumn/Winter 2005
France-Amérique, Paris, 3 March 2005, 6.00 p.m.

The term *genometrics* describes the biometric analyses of chromosomes and stresses the application of statistical methods to the study of genomic data. 'The collection evolved from the idea of how different individuals living in London would fit into London life depending on the reaction of their DNA sequences to the London soundscape through a specifically developed programme,' Chalayan explained. 'Each letter of their DNA sequence was mapped out on the garment and "sensitized" to react to different sounds which make up the soundscape. The shapes seen within the animation were frozen at a peak point in action creating the basis for design.' Tapestry elements, shaved carpet weaves in coated cottons and jumbo corduroys were used to give life to the impressive sculptural shapes taken directly from the sound test experiments. DNA as a theme is also used by Chalayan in his 2005 film *Absence Presence. Pamela Golbin.*

Hussein Chalayan_Garment Deformer/04Output

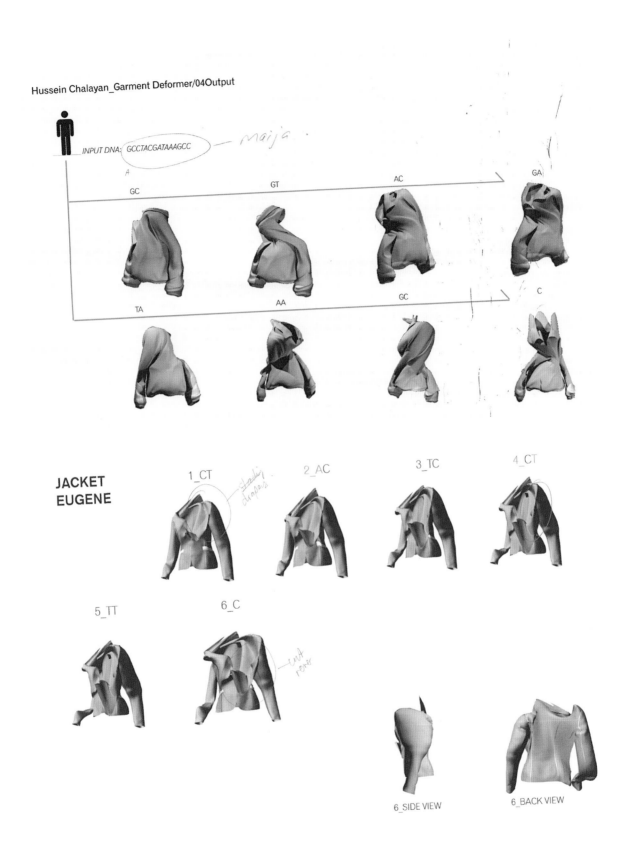

Development plans and sketches for
Genometrics, Autumn/Winter 2000.
Courtesy Hussein Chalayan.

ABOVE RIGHT:
A look from *Genometrics*, Autumn/Winter 2005,
exhibited at the Museum of Contemporary Art, Tokyo,
3 April to 20 June 2010.
Photograph by Keizo Kioku.

OPPOSITE AND ABOVE LEFT:
Genometrics, Autumn/Winter 2005.
Show photographs by Chris Moore.

MIRAGE

Autumn/Winter 2010
Couvent des Cordeliers, Paris, 7 March 2010, 3.00 p.m.

With *Mirage*, Chalayan continued to reinterpret the idea of the 'journey' – literal and metaphorical, physical and transcendental. The collection evolved from the concept of an American road trip and how a journey can shape a woman's wardrobe. He noted: 'I am interested in identifying the details that bind a garment to a location and the dialogue between identity and place, which are ongoing themes in my work. The archetypal representation of The American Road Trip appealed to me greatly, as it offered a rich source of inspiration to drive the exploration of this theme further.' Across a diverse array of states and terrains, from city to sea, through mountains and over deserts, the journey begins in New York then looks to the Pennsylvania Amish community for inspiration. The glamour of Texan beauty pageants was present in elements such as sashes twisted and trapped between layers of encrusted lace and chiffon, draped as if they had encountered a hurricane, which are common in the area. The proximity of Texas to the Mexican border was hinted at through use of bright wools in red, lilac and yellow that had been knitted to form ruffles, or intricately crocheted. A leather hat and caplet combination connote the exploration of the great expanses of Utah. Arriving in Hollywood, Chalayan evoked 'the elegance of Silver Screen starlets with floor-length black crepe dresses split to the thigh and invaded with pleated inserts that become a conceptual interpretation of the red-carpet gown.' *Pamela Golbin.*

Mirage

OPPOSITE:
Studio montage for the 'journey' in the collection
Mirage, Autumn/Winter 2010.

ABOVE AND THE FOLLOWING PAGES:
Mirage, Autumn/Winter 2010.
Show photographs by Chris Moore.

OPPOSITE:
Vogue magazine (UK), October 2010.
Photograph by Paul Wetherell / *Vogue* / The Condé Nast Publications Ltd.
Model: Lily Donaldson.

ABOVE:
Mirage, Autumn/Winter 2010.
Show photographs by Chris Moore.

NEW YORK
'WALKING ON THIN ICE' BY YOKO ONO

PENNSYLVANIA
'APPALACHIAN SPRING' BY AARON COPLAND

TEXAS
'TRUCKIN' BY GRATEFUL DEAD
'YOU'RE GONNA MISS ME' BY THE 13TH-FLOOR ELEVATORS
'FARE THEE WELL, MISS CAROUSEL' BY TOWNES VAN ZANDT
'WHEN I GROW OLD' BY MICHELLE SHOCKED
'GOIN' DOWN TO MEXICO' BY ZZ TOP

MEXICO
'EL CUMBANCHERO' BY SABU MARTINEZ
'ESPERANZA' BY LOS MANCHUCAMBOS

UTAH
'RUN TO YOU' BY BRYAN ADAMS
'EZY RYDER' BY JIMI HENDRIX
'ROCK YOUR BODY' BY JUSTIN TIMBERLAKE
'SYMPHONY NO.2' BY CHARLES IVES

L A
'TAKE PILLS' BY PANDA BEAR
'ELEPHANTS' BY WARPAINT
'DREAM BROTHER' BY JEFF BUCKLEY

Track list of music for *Mirage*, Autumn/Winter 2010.
Show photographs by Chris Moore.

THE
ART
OF
BALANCE

Rebecca Lowthorpe

Hussein Chalayan is determined that his commercial collaborations should be written about in this book. And I must confess that I inwardly groaned when he asked me to write this chapter. Of all the Chalayan topics – the rich tapestry of ideas, the Turkish Cypriot roots so deeply embedded in his work, the emotionally charged shows – design consultancies would probably feature last on my list of things to find fascinating about Hussein.

But then I think about what he's achieved – and that there is even a book at all, celebrating a body of work that spans nearly 20 years – and realise that perhaps the most remarkable thing about Hussein is that he is still here, still creating on his terms. The reason for this – and it might be the most artistic thing he's ever done – is that he managed to make a business out of his art.

You have no idea how surprising this is unless you've known him from the beginning. I met Hussein in September 1989 during one of our first few days at Central Saint Martins School of Art. He stood out. Not because he'd wear a pale blue jacket and on occasion darken a beauty spot on his chin – there were far more outrageous looks to behold than his – but because he had no qualms about talking to anybody, students or tutors, and extracting from them the most intimate of personal details. Unlike the rest of us who hid behind a veil of aloofness, Hussein had no reserve whatsoever, no stop-valve either; he had a desire to know everything about everybody. And while some treated his well-meant inquisitiveness with disdain, I embraced it. Coming from rural Lincolnshire – a wannabe fashion journalist – this exotic Cypriot was precisely the kind of eccentric nut I'd always imagined I'd find at London's eminent fashion school. Like some kind of mystic, he would look into your face and tell you how 'viking' you were, or 'Byzantine' and then swiftly proceed to the subject of your mother: Was yours a good relationship? Were you close? And what did it feel like to have sisters? A lonely only child, he seemed to be looking for siblings.

He never assumed the airs of a fashion designer – that was the main difference between him and his student peers. While they looked and acted much more like the real thing and seemed to have contacts and knowledge of the industry, Hussein, fond as he was of the more avant-garde designers Martin Margiela and Rei Kawakubo, seemed too caught up in his own head to be able to look outward. I never pictured him as a fashion designer – a sculptor maybe or an architect seemed the more likely result. Not that he didn't shine in the pattern-cutting room, where he demonstrated an uncanny ability to visualise complicated flat paper patterns in three dimensions. I remember watching him construct from a long rectangle of white paper, criss-crossed with fine pencil marks, an origami neck ruff; it looked part Elizabethan part extra-terrestrial space craft.

He wasn't some kind of conceptualist leader who outsmarted everyone else. The truth of it is that he was one of a clutch of gifted students who found inspiration way beyond the world of fashion – chemistry compositions, radio components, aircraft manufacturing were par for the course. The fact that it was such a competitive hotbed of conceptual design only made him burrow more deeply into his theory books. It wasn't until he graduated in 1993 with his cause célèbre collection – famously burying it in his friend Sharon's back garden to see how it would decompose – that he pulled rank and confirmed his place as Central Saint Martins' chief avant-garde theorist. Soon after, the collection was celebrated in Brown's boutique window, but even then the idea of him manufacturing a line of clothes that anybody might actually want to wear – much less run a business – seemed way out of his scope.

In September 1999, six years after we graduated, *The Guardian* sent me to New York to interview Hussein about his collaboration with the high-end cashmere company, TSE. It seemed strange that a low-key, multi-million dollar global commercial operation such as TSE should have picked an avant-garde British designer to take it into the next century, even in the context of the late 1990s when long-established fashion houses were snapping up star designers to rejuvenate their brands and grab the headlines. At that time John Galliano was ensconced at Dior, Alexander

McQueen at Givenchy, Marc Jacobs at Louis Vuitton and Michael Kors at Celine. This, after all, was the designer who had become famous for collections like his yashmak 'nudes', giant wooden pod heads and the *Remote-control Dress*. I asked TSE's then creative director, Rebecca Shafer, why she had chosen Hussein: 'Fashion has moved away from designers who are great stylists to those who actually design,' she said, adding, 'We wanted Hussein's unique point of view.'

The Spring/Summer 2000 collection for the TSE New York line, called *Shadows*, was his fourth for the company and the second to be shown on the catwalk. He described the collection at the time as 'trapped clothes with an element of trompe l'oeil, like echoes of light when you're filming in the background'. The clothes had the same sparse, linear quality of the most simple pieces he might have made for his own line, except that they were a little more colourful and feminine, cut from the most superior double-faced cashmeres, a material he couldn't afford to use back in London. He talked about how much he was learning from the newest technology and experienced technicians. With TSE, his first exposure to a professional environment outside his own, Hussein saw the inner workings of a commercial brand – for the first time he was working with marketing, merchandising and sales teams. It was the 'response mechanisms' that TSE used that really turned him on, meaning that the company could track every style, size and colour that had been sold anywhere in the world. Far from feeling alienated by this commercial 'evidence', Hussein revelled in the immediate feedback of his performance and used the information to help him build his collections accordingly. He also enjoyed the 'range planning' aspect of the job – the way a collection has to relate to its retail environment. TSE even took him on trunk shows, in-store presentations where he got the opportunity to talk his designs through with prospective customers. In Los Angeles and San Francisco, he came face-to-face with real clients – something he had never been able to do with his own line. He couldn't believe that he might be talking to a 20-year-old one minute and a 60-year-old the next, that they

FIG. 2–6

FIG. I

FIG. 7–I2

FIG. I–I2
TSE New York collections by Hussein Chalayan:
Autumn/Winter 1998 (I);
Spring/Summer 1999 (2–6);
Autumn/Winter 1999 (7–12).
Photographs by Dan Lecca.

FIG. 13-16

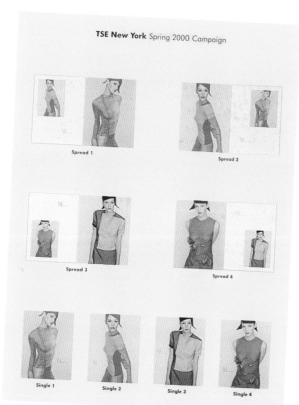

FIG. 18-19

FIG. 17

FIG. 20-22

FIG. 13-22:
TSE New York collections by Hussein Chalayan:
Spring/Summer 2000 (13-17);
Autumn/Winter 2000 (18-19);
Spring/Summer 2001 (20-22).

were all shapes, sizes and types of people fascinated him. He noted how he could influence their perception of the clothes and ultimately how rewarding it was to have first-hand experience of selling – even today, he says this is one of his 'most cherished experiences'.

'New York made me feel that anything was possible,' he says, looking back to that time. 'There was this enterprising, positive energy that was really refreshing. I think it's the one place other than London that I could have lived and I did toy with the idea of moving there.'

'I really treated TSE like it was my own collection,' he continues. 'It wasn't lesser in any way. To be honest, there were ideas that crossed over, like the *Shadows* collection, I was also interested in doing it for my own line but in the end I didn't pursue it. But yes, there's a constant play with ideas, whether I can do it for myself or not as well, so it's sometimes hard, because you're only one person you can only have so many ideas. The thing is, TSE wasn't conceptual, I hate the word conceptual, but my work had a real narrative at the time and TSE would be one idea. It had less recognisable cultural elements than what I did for myself, so it was much more of a graphic exercise.'

After six seasons, just over three years, the collaboration came to an end. Flying long haul every month to New York had taken its toll and the management at the company changed several times. 'The result of that was that there were a lot of people not getting on with each other any more and that made me feel uncomfortable,' he says.

While his work for TSE didn't exactly add much in the way of dynamism to the Hussein Chalayan oeuvre, it ultimately proved that he could cut it in the commercial world. So when in the late 1990s and early 2000s he was creating some of his most ambitious collections and memorable shows under his own name (much of it financed by his consulting fee from TSE), the industry was constantly reminded that he could also make simple, wearable, saleable clothes. This played well with the Americans, and in particular American *Vogue*'s Anna Wintour, the fashion industry's most powerful editor in chief, who was to play chief strategist in his next move.

In 2000, Wintour introduced Hussein to Lawrence Stroll, a Canadian retail magnate who, together with Silas Chou, a Hong-Kong-based textile and apparel manufacturer, had acquired the Queen's jewellers, Asprey & Garrard. The following year, at Wintour's insistence, Hussein was hired as the director of fashion for Asprey. Except that there was no fashion at Asprey. Hussein's role, therefore, was to create a fashion department from scratch – to hire his own team of designers to work on shoes, accessories, menswear, womenswear, knitwear, fabric and, in so doing, create a whole Asprey 'lifestyle'. Far from being overwhelmed by the scale of the project, all he could see was the potential to do something exciting, and all of it a long way from anything he'd done before. 'I wanted it to be a James Bond product,' he says. 'Here was this institution, this very British House, with this incredible archive – amazing items, like cigarette holders, that would have a quirk to them in the way they opened – and I thought I could give that a modern angle. The idea of doing a parka, say, that's transformable but looks completely traditional from the outside, felt like such an exciting next step for me.'

But sadly, the project, which lasted three years, never lived up to its potential. Although many products were eventually made and delivered to the shop floor, they were never publicised with any conviction. There were no catwalk shows, no showroom presentations, I don't remember seeing a single press release showing the fruits of Hussein's labour. 'The trouble with Asprey was that they had a Canadian majority stakeholder [Stroll] who had hired an Italian chief executive and it was supposed to be a British company,' he explains. 'And I felt stuck between these two people from two different cultures who, in my view, didn't share the same vision with each other or me.'

Asprey was also a loss in the financial sense. Almost every penny of Hussein's design consultancy was funnelled back into the making of his own line. Mercifully, a white knight was waiting in the wings in the form of Franco Pene,

Asprey collection by Hussein Chalayan,
Vogue magazine (US), December 2003.
Photograph by Raymond Meier/trunkarchive.com.
Model: Hana Soukupova.

FIG. 23-26

FIG. 27-30

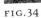
FIG. 34

FIG. 31-33

FIG. 23-34:
Chalayan second line collections:
Autumn/Winter 2006 (23-26). Photographs by Daniel Jackson.
Autumn/Winter 2007 (27-30). Photographs Simeon Coates.
Spring/Summer 2008 (31-33). Photographs courtesy Hussein Chalayan.
Spring/Summer 2005 (34). Photograph by Timur Celikdag.

an Italian manufacturer whose company, Gibo, had produced the likes of Alexander McQueen and Viktor & Rolf. For years, Hussein had been talking about whether or not to go into business with Mr Pene and the timing seemed right to embark on a licensing deal. Hussein was ready to make a second more commercial line, using strands of his past mainline concepts, and also branch into menswear. Not doing Asprey any more meant that he was free to focus on his new venture. Also, by this point, Hussein had become the go-to fashion designer for the art world; so projects for galleries and museums as well as limited editions of his films, provided another smaller, yet vital, stream of revenue. (To put this in perspective, by June 2004, his fashion work and films had been featured in or the sole subject of more than 30 exhibitions – the figure more than doubles by 2011).

The second line, *Chalayan*, and the menswear were a commercial success, appealing to both men for the first time and women who hadn't been able to afford the catwalk-shown collection. And by 2008, Pene proposed an even closer arrangement, to take a stake in the trademark of the Hussein Chalayan label. But into the ring stepped Puma, the sports and lifestyle brand owned by the French conglomerate, PPR (Pinault-Printemps-Redoute), one of whose subsidiaries is the Gucci Group which owns Gucci, Yves Saint Laurent, Stella McCartney, Alexander McQueen and Balenciaga, among others. The Puma offer, led by the chief executive, Jochen Zeitz, wasn't just more financially lucrative – on top of becoming a creative director in charge of two of Puma's lines, the company would also invest in the Hussein Chalayan business and allow him to use the Gucci manufacturing facilities. It was impossible to turn the deal down, but it required a team of lawyers and much nail biting before he could extract himself from his licensing arrangement with Mr Pene. Soon after, a team of six designers were drafted in to work full time on Puma, giving Chalayan's East End studio for the first time the air of a business-like operation. He says it was necessary to have an on-site, dedicated team

because the Puma corporation, the biggest corporation he's ever dealt with, is so de-centred, meaning there is not one central headquarters, but division upon division, with bases all over the world.

Puma was about 'reaching more people' with his name, so the lines he oversees – 'Urban Mobility' and 'Shala' – are both co-branded with Hussein Chalayan. The first is performance related sportswear, the second 'more of a yoga-type line, you can work out in it and go for a coffee as well'. Both, I imagine, to be a million sartorial miles away from his own-name line.

Above all, it is the technology aspect of Puma that so appeals to Hussein – always such a great source of inspiration, he now has the opportunity to see some of his more technological ideas come to fruition, and on a global commercial scale. 'Remember the *Speedstruck* dresses at the end of the *Inertia* show (Spring/Summer 2009) Well I've done a shoe like that, a running shoe, that takes that shape, well, a calmer version of it,' he says, delighted to explain how it was created by way of 3D modelling. 'That it's going to become a commercial product is really exciting because often my ideas like that remained as prototypes; so the fact that it's going to be produced in different colours, different sizes... It means that those things I've been developing for years can now, through Puma, reach people. So that for me is very rewarding.'

To hear Hussein talk about 'price-driven product' and 'value for money items' and 'brand visibility', only reiterates how far he's come. That he is as genuinely interested, excited and inspired by the process as he ever was, says as much about his un-cynical nature as it does about keeping his design integrity intact. It doesn't seem to bother him too much that Puma pulled out their investment in his company soon after the global financial crisis, in 2009. His contract as a creative director there doesn't run out until 2014 and who knows it may be renewed. Or perhaps he will find another outlet for turning his art into commerce. Whatever happens, I am looking forward to Hussein Chalayan's next step.

PUMA

FIG.35-37

FIG.38-39

FIG.40-41

FIG.42-44

FIG.45

FIG.46-47

FIG.35-47:
Puma collection by Hussein Chalayan,
Autumn/Winter 2011.
Photographs by Benjamin Alexander Huseby,
Magnus Unnar (38-39) and Ben Weller (46-47).

FIG. 48-49

FIG. 50-51

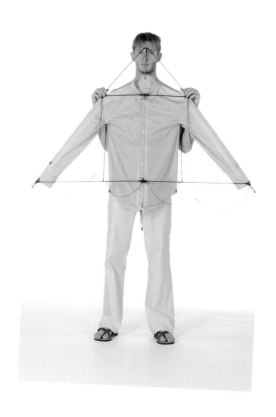

FIG. 52-53

FIG. 48-53:
Temporal Meditations (menswear), Spring/Summer 2004 (48-49).
Anthropology of Solitude (menswear), Autumn/Winter 2004 (50-51).
Act to Institution (menswear), Spring/Summer 2005 (52-53).
Photographs courtesy Hussein Chalayan.

FIG. 54-57

FIG. 61-62

FIG. 58-60

FIG. 63-67

FIG. 54-67:
In Shadows (menswear), Autumn/Winter 2005 (54-57).
Touch Wood (menswear), Spring/Summer 2006 (58-62).
Anamorphics (menswear), Autumn/Winter 2006 (63-67).
Photographs courtesy Hussein Chalayan.

A SYNOPTIC GUIDE TO
HUSSEIN CHALAYAN'S MAINLINE COLLECTIONS 1993-2011

Pamela Golbin

The following descriptions of shows by Hussein Chalayan, from his 1993 graduation show to Spring/Summer 2011, were written by the author to be read both individually, as they appear throughout this book, and as a continuous text, as collected here. Statements by Chalayan have been sourced from interviews with Golbin, from the catalogue for his 2010 Istanbul Modern exhibition or from the designer's own press releases.

THE TANGENT FLOWS (p. 29) *July 1993*
Central Saint Martins graduation collection
The Clapham Grand, Clapham Junction, London
Hussein Chalayan's graduation collection from Central Saint Martins set the groundwork for his intricate creative process. Strictly personal and often biographical, the complex narratives used by Chalayan are powerful tools that assist him in his design approach. For *The Tangent Flows*, Chalayan based his thesis collection on the duality of spirit and matter, researching the works of Isaac Newton and René Descartes, as well as Carl Jung. Chalayan explained his early collection: 'It was about the life of a scientist trying to integrate Eastern philosophy into the Western Cartesian worldview, and the revolts she encountered in her journey. There is a dance which takes place in the story where performers with interactive magnetized clothing (symbolizing the quest of the scientist) have iron filings thrown at them in the form of a protest, they then get kidnapped, murdered and buried with their clothes intact. I then re-enacted this action and buried clothes from this imaginary dance performance with iron filings on them, which later I showed with segments of text from the story relating to what happened to the dancers as labels in the clothes.' Although the narrative systems Chalayan puts into place allow him to release his ideas, he is conscious that as a fashion designer the final result is in clothes. He stated: 'I think processes are there for the designer. The result is the important thing for the people and they don't have to know the process.'

CARTESIA (p. 32) *Autumn/Winter 1994*
Grosvenor Gallery, London, 29 March 1994, 6.00 p.m.
For his first commercial collection, Chalayan developed the narrative of his graduation work, insofar as he remained interested, he said, in Cartesian 'influences over nationalism and fragmentation as an essence of war. The way in which the body becomes anonymous within war. The dead emulated by documents, symbolised by a series of paper garments in contradictory bright celebratory colours, airmail signs illustrating the way in which they could be sent to their places of origin'. He explained his process: 'I used real paper at first. Then I wanted to find something indestructible, so I used Tyvek, which is artificial paper.' Chalayan referenced aerogrammes – which he remembers using in childhood – to create dresses with the airmail letters' distinct folds. The aged and decomposed 'buried dresses' were again presented as an antithesis to the white crisp paper of the *Airmail* clothing.

TEMPORARY INTERFERENCE ⌢ (p. 52) *Spring/Summer 1995*
British Fashion Council Tent, Natural History Museum,
London, 9 October 1994, 6.15 p.m.
For *Temporary Interference*, Chalayan created a board game in which the notion of God as the weather interferes temporarily with our daily lives. The designer said: 'It was a fictional game... about the hierarchy of God and man and about how we see God as a separate entity. That for me is Cartesian philosophy.' The act of throwing the dice controlled what would happen to the clothes. Whatever direction one took in the game, the result was always that one had to jump off a great height in order to reach the Divine. The balloons worn by the models were to assist in their ascension to the heavens, but they inevitably fell short of their destination symbolizing, for Chalayan, the fallacies of religion and its contradictions as well as the 'absurdity demonstrated by jumping off bridge heights in the hope of being saved by an exterior force'. 'Buried dresses' are shown

in various states of decomposition after falling from flight into a river, or more symbolically, after falling from grace.

ALONG FALSE EQUATOR ⌢ (p. 55) *Autumn/Winter 1995*
British Fashion Council Tent, Natural History Museum,
London, 12 March 1995, 6.30 p.m.
Airline routes, cardiograms, meteorological charts and photographic landscapes are all used as prints and decorative elements in this collection which explored the notion of being in transit while simultaneously being omnipresent. Chalayan uses 'travel as a means of exploring the external world and the world within'. LED lights represented flashing airport lights. Flight paths printed onto the clothes created an atlas embodying a sense of constant movement. Printed neoprene (the material used in scuba diving clothes) evoked a change of environment and the urgency of an aeroplane's takeoff. At a time when globalisation issues were just beginning to emerge, Chalayan explored travel as a means of attaining ubiquity since the body can physically be anywhere, a state that he described as, 'an inhuman mechanic materiality that can tear away your skin'.

NOTHING, INTERSCOPE ♀ (p. 198) *Spring/Summer 1996*
Bagleys Warehouse, London, 21 October 1995, 6.00 p.m.
The biblical stories of Noah's Ark and Armageddon inspired Chalayan for this collection. He explained: 'Through narrative, I try to create a look for the body that represents an event.' For *Nothing, Interscope*, Chalayan explored the question: 'If a natural disaster struck the world, how would you react to it?' Originally, the collection was to be shown in a flooded church. Surgical corsets worn over skirts offered an idea of how the body could be reconstructed after a flood or disaster. To create an indelible image that would resist such a catastrophe, Chalayan stated: 'I asked Wakako Kishimoto to paint flowers, which for me, is a universally beautiful thing and it's timeless. We fed her hand-painted patterns to the computer and pixalized them.' Thus preserving her design forever through the digitalization. 'I used Hokusai waves on dresses to represent destruction, the end of the world.' Small sticks to hold the models' lips apart allude to Christian religious paintings depicting the open mouths of bodies ascending to heaven.

STILL LIFE *(not illustrated) Autumn/Winter 1996*
British Fashion Council Tent, Natural History Museum,
London, March 1996
With *Still Life*, Chalayan continued to develop his creative vocabulary and explore the notion of character while creating a sense that, in his designs, the body is representative of a state of mind or state of being. The show's invitation depicted a cinema curtain, which represented, 'how we frame things when we look at them'. He took his cues from Hollywood and its femme fatale heroines. Chalayan explored the genre of film noire, with a touch of vampire gothic, to create the attitudes of *Still Life*'s strong, confident women. Like a still life, each model turned on a revolving platform and took the pose of a freeze-framed image. The prints were graphic with art deco elements. Inspired by idea of watching movies, tweed jackets with leather piping had little belts that could attach to a chair – a way for the clothes to embody the cinematic feeling.

LANDS WITHOUT ✎ (p. 174) *Spring/Summer 1997*
Riverside Studios, London, 28 September 1996, 7.45 p.m.
For *Lands Without*, Chalayan drew his inspiration from women's roles in German fairy tales and their portrayal as scapegoat figures. 'I wanted to look at fairy tales because they portray a certain amount of horror,' Chalayan stated. Literary influences from the novels of British writer Marina Warner and the infamous 15th-century treatise on witchcraft, *Malleus Maleficarum*, served as references in the collection's development. Chalayan's focus in the tale of *Rapunzel* was the character's long blond

hair, which connected, for him, to an Aryan sense of empowerment. Chalayan noted: 'I use her hair as kite strings so that [Rapunzel] can escape her tower by flying out.' The title *Lands Without* is taken from Jean-Luc Godard's 1965 film *Alphaville*, whose heroine tries to escape an imposed predicament.

SCENT OF TEMPESTS ⌣ (p. 59) *Autumn/Winter 1997*
Atlantis Gallery, London, 27 February 1997, 4.30 p.m.
For Chalayan, *Scent of Tempests* inaugurated a new chapter in his design process, in which his narrative became more abstract as he attempted to create a wardrobe in relation to a religious belief system. 'Often I find that people who worship pray for bad things not to happen,' Chalayan observed. *Scent of Tempests* warns of an impending disaster, an explosion in the waiting. After designing his collection *Temporary Interference* (Spring/Summer 1995), external forces were again incarnated by the weather. In *Scent of Tempests* this took the form a god that was part of nature, punctuating our daily lives. The designer's intention was to create appropriate attire for worship. Although the jewellery in the collection could have Islamic connotations, Chalayan used it as a decorative element to adorn the devotee in his veneration just as the embroidered fans – which were also part of the collection – served to embellish and protect the wearer.

BETWEEN ⌣ (p. 61) *Spring/Summer 1998*
Atlantis Gallery, London, 27 September 1997, 8.15 p.m.
A natural continuation of *Scent of Tempests*, the collection *Between* further explored the notion of worship and deconstructed how we define our territory through belief systems. During the creative process of designing the collection, Chalayan asked nude models to stake out an area on a beach in Dungeness, East Sussex, using ropes and poles, thus defining their territory. Once the physical space was marked out, Chalayan explored and questioned the notion of identity which can easily be erased by the concealment of one's face. Models dressed in red wore egg-shaped capsules that entirely covered their faces, offering a certain protection from the gaze of others but completely removing any sense of their individuality and eliminating their personality. Others wore headpieces framed in mirrors that allowed the spectators to see and be seen in their reflection. The show ended with six models dressed in black chadors of varying lengths. The first walked out completely naked, wearing only a minute yashmak that hid her face. The following models wore chadors that increasingly concealed their nude bodies. Controversial but not confrontational, Chalayan was interested in showing how through 'the religious code you are depersonified'.

PANORAMIC ♟ (p. 200) *Autumn/Winter 1998*
Atlantis Gallery, London, 24 February 1998, 8.00 p.m.
With *Panoramic*, Chalayan explored language and its limitations. He explained: 'I looked at the idea of how you define things through language and I wanted to create things that you couldn't describe…' The starting point for the collection was provided by Ludwig Wittgenstein's *Tractatus*, in which the Austrian philosopher argues: 'Whereof we cannot speak, thereof we must be silent.' The limits of language become the limits of thought. Chalayan also expressed that he wanted 'to create a new uniform that couldn't be described,' where the body was lost in parameters that are mostly man-made. Part ethnic costume, part uniform, Chalayan created hybrid garments that camouflaged the individual to blend in with his surroundings resulting in dire anonymity. Mirrors were an important element in the show providing several different and simultaneous views or echoes of reality, exploring both the individual's and the spectator's physical territory as well as their respective roles. Chalayan concluded the show with models holding large coloured building blocks, which were the same colours as the pixellated landscape image projected at the show and that, for Chalayan, symbolized basic elements for constructing everyday reality.

GEOTROPICS ◣ (p. 236) *Spring/Summer 1999*
Atlantis Gallery, London, 28 September 1998, 8.30 p.m.
A biological term, *geotropics* refers to the oriented growth of an organism with respect to the force of gravity. Integrating the notion of nature and its forces, Chalayan's collection *Geotropics* reflected upon the role of natural topographical features, such as mountains and rivers, as well as human actions, such as wars, in shaping the definition of a nation. Chalayan used the body to create a micro-geography. In a computer-animated film, he brought together national costumes from different places and eras along the 2000-year-old Silk Route which extends from China to the West. The film was a journey through time and space, morphing garments from one to another. Two monumental dresses were presented in the finale. In one, head and armrests constituted a chair that was integrated into the model's clothing forming the silhouette and its wearer into a single and unique entity.

ECHOFORM ♟ (p. 90) *Autumn/Winter 1999*
Playscape Go-Kart Centre, London, 24 February 1999, 7.30 p.m.
For his last three collections, Chalayan has explored the definition of barriers, whether physical, linguistic or geographical. With *Echoform*, Chalayan probed the notion of speed and its relation to the body – whether it is used to propel the body forward through technological advances or as a reflective force. 'Everything we do is an amplification of the body,' Chalayan noted recently. 'And I thought why not look at those things and then project them back into the body.' Cars and aeroplanes were the direct inspiration for the collection, materializing the man-made machines that best symbolize speed. Chairs, headrests and streamlining were integrated into the structure of the garments. Leather padded headrests or neck cushions accessorised the dresses and echoed the form froms which they are derived. Chalayan presented a second version of his *Aeroplane Dress* made of fibreglass and resin cast into an aircraft form. Operated electronically, the skirt integrated flaps that can extend just like the wings of a plane.

BEFORE MINUS NOW ♟ (p. 94) *Spring/Summer 2000*
Sadler's Wells Theatre, London, 23 September 1999, 8.00 p.m.
In *Before Minus Now*, Chalayan focused on invisible forces as a means to construct form. The designer was particularly interested in phenomena that become visible entities. He explored the powers of expansion, magnetism and erosion and how these can be applied to garments in order to create shape. To express expansion, Chalayan used heat to modify the shape of a flared red dress. Harking back to the 1950s New Look silhouette, Chalayan's take on the feminine dress was inflated on stage where it unfolded and amplified in volume. Then, Chalayan's fibreglass, remote-control *Aeroplane Dress* was transformed with the touch of a button. The body was consequently metamorphosed through an artificial, man-made force that combined the elements of magnetism and technological advances. To embody the action of erosion, Chalayan shaved a bale of shapeless pink tulle giving it the contour of a dress. In the same way that the formation of mountains occurs through natural erosion, Chalayan formed his own monuments through the gradual cutting of the fabric. In the finale, five models were presented, wearing deconstructed corsets in vivid colours with matching pleated skirts. With these designs, Chalayan paid tribute to the natural force of the wind as a powerful tool that can alter and create forms.

AFTERWORDS ◣ (p. 242) *Autumn/Winter 2000*
Sadler's Wells Theatre, London, 16 February 2000, 8.30 p.m.
Inspired by the plight of the refugee and the horror of being displaced in times of war, *Afterwords* makes reference to how Turkish Cypriots were subjected to ethnic cleansing in Cyprus prior to the division of the island in 1974. Chalayan revealed: 'This project started off from the war in Kosovo and then I connected it to what happened in Cyprus which was quite similar, when Greek EOKA sympathizers, in an attempt to unite Cyprus to Greece, were terrorizing Turkish Cypriot homes.' In this collection, Chalayan explored the reactions of people who are confronted by war and their need to hide their possessions or to carry them on their exodus. Chalayan staged his collection in a minimal white space that was set up like a living room, with four sitting room chairs, a table, a flat-screen television and an object-filled shelf. First, an average family walked on stage: mother, father, grandmother and children. Then from a hidden door, models appeared in seemingly simple clothes and began to seize, one by one, the objects in the room, fitting them into special pockets in their garments designed to contain them. Finally, models wearing simple grey shift dresses entered, removed the chair covers and proceeded to put them on. One last model, stepped inside the wooden table and pulled it up her legs and waist, transforming it into a voluminous skirt. The chairs

were folded up to become suitcases and the models exited the set. The white room was left completely empty and lifeless.

VENTRILOQUY ͝ (p. 72) *Spring/Summer 2001*
Gainsborough Studios, London, 27 September 2000, 8.00 p.m.
Held in a studio where Alfred Hitchcock shot several feature films, *Ventriloquy* began with a computer-animated film in which a 3D female figure (delineated in wire-frame-like lines) ruthlessly shatters another figure into thousands of pieces, to reflect, Chalayan said, 'how value systems collapse at times of war.' After this virtual interaction, the real models appeared on a white set with a geometrical grid that echoed the one in the animated film. From the chaos of destruction and to music provided by the Jupiter Orchestra, conducted by Gregory Rose, emerged a silhouette of spare topstitched suits, loose shift dresses and intricately pleated, voluminous skirts. Prints of red poppies alluded not only to the flowers' distinctive attribute of thriving in difficult environments but also to their use as a symbol commemorating soldiers killed in action. In the dramatic finale of the presentation, Chalayan sent out six models. Three of them held small mallets with which they smashed their companions' fragile sugar-glass garments, exposing their stark nakedness and mirroring the actions of their alter egos seen previously in the film by Chalayan.

MAPREADING ♀ (p. 212) *Autumn/Winter 2001*
Chalayan's *Mapreading* collection opened a new chapter in his design process. Particularly demanding technically, *Mapreading* used 'morphing' techniques to transform each garment in the collection. Like film stills, each silhouette smoothly faded into the next, differing only slightly from the preceding one to recount the mini life-span of a contemporary wardrobe. Beginning with a black coat, all of the classics were accounted for – from the little black dress to the white shirt, the jacket, the denim jacket and finally a version of the 'buried dress'. The decomposed dress crystallized the ravages of time and ended the cycle. But with decay ultimately comes rebirth: the cycle's revival was thus guaranteed. For Chalayan, *Mapreading* was the root of his Spring/Summer 2007 collection, *One Hundred and Eleven*, in which five hand-constructed, mechanically engineered dresses morph from one era to another.

MEDEA ͝ (p. 76) *Spring/Summer 2002*
Couvent des Cordeliers, Paris, 5 October 2001, 8.00 p.m.
Inspired by a *Dictionary of Superstition*, Chalayan uses the sorceress Medea and her magical powers as the central figure of this collection. 'The design is a wish or a curse that casts the garment and its wearer in a time warp through historical periods, like a sudden tumble through the sediment of an archaeological dig,' Chalayan explained. Through elaborate seaming and detailing, the garments were built up in various layers of silks and cottons. They have been deconstructed, sometimes tattered, twisted and ripped to represent the wishes and/or curses. Thus, the altered conditions of the garments symbolize a hexed state. 'The garment is a ghost of all the multiple lives it may have had,' Chalayan continued. 'Nothing is shiny and new; everything has a history... Thus a 1960s dress gets cut-away to reveal its past as a medieval dress; or, in reverse, a Victorian corset gets cut away to reveal a modern jersey vest; a 1930s dress gets cut away to disclose its past as an Edwardian dress.' As a *clin d'oeil* to the work presented at his college graduation show, Chalayan buried and aged some of the dresses of the finale.

AMBIMORPHOUS ☼ (p. 128) *Autumn/Winter 2002*
Cité de la Musique, Paris, 8 March 2002, 9.00 p.m.
In Chalayan's 2003 statement for his Mode Museum, Antwerp, exhibition, the designer explained: 'The aim of this project is to explore the shady territory between realism and surrealism, power and powerlessness. As an example, I intend to examine the connections between *Alice in Wonderland* as a representation of a surreal entity, and war as a real life force.' To illustrate his theme of power and powerlessness, in part, Chalayan's models walked out through props of differing scales, to make them seem oversize on one end of the runway and diminutive on the other. He began the show by sending out a lone Asian model dressed in a richly embroidered traditional costume from Eastern Turkey. Other models followed wearing designs with 'ethnic' detailing as increasingly black coloured 'Western' skirts and pantsuits

completely usurped the original costume. The morphing then was reversed. From all-black silhouettes, the ethnic detailing once again was slowly integrated, and the last piece was the costume that began the show. 'The clothes represent forms that are so-called "ambimorphous" where all forms can morph in two different directions...'

MANIFEST DESTINY ✐ (p. 175) *Spring/Summer 2003*
Salle Gaveau, Paris, 4 October 2002, 8.00 p.m.
Manifest Destiny refers to the doctrine deployed in the middle of the 19th century to legitimize America's urge for expansion. Chalayan observed: 'I am interested in the psychological and the physical implications of imperial expansion, the way in which this force attempts to civilize our animal state... In *Manifest Destiny* I wanted to look at the body in its anatomical state and how clothes which cover, adorn and control could recultivate and reappropriate anatomy, perhaps at times to an unrecognizable extent disguising all notions of "disgust".' With anatomy as a starting point, Chalayan explored the meaning of clothes that have been used to cover, lace-up or deform the body and how these standards can impose Western ideologies. By using Lycra-infused materials, Chalayan draped the body, liberating it from constraints through the fabrics' elasticity. He presented a collection of constructed and deconstructed garments with complex cut-outs and revealing mini-dresses in abstract prints. The finale dresses offered 'decorative holes' revealing the abdominal area as if organs had been ripped out leaving nothing but strips of skin. The music for this show was provided by The Brood, a band directed by musician Susan Stenger, with choreographer Michael Clark, artist Cerith Wyn Evans and Chalayan himself performing live on bass guitars.

KINSHIP JOURNEYS ͝ (p. 80) *Autumn/Winter 2003*
Théâtre de Paris, Paris, 7 March 2003, 8.30 p.m.
With *Kinship Journeys*, Chalayan commented on the practices of the Roman Catholic church and the meaning of hope, sin and salvation in our lives. Chalayan explained: 'The collection was in three parts, each monument on stage related to each section. The first part (the trampoline) represented the idea of trying to reach the divine with the balloons attached to dresses as if they were to enhance the upward movement. The second part represented the way in which we allow our sins and guilt to rule our lives. Hence, after your confession you would plant a seed within a drawer of the confessional that contained soil and your sins would manifest themselves as fruit or flowers. The final part, evolving around the coffin boat, is perhaps a comment on resisting death.' First presented by Chalayan in his Spring/Summer 1995 collection, suspended balloons were used as an artifice to elevate the model to the 'Divine' for a deliverance that will not occur. Dresses, jackets and coats were built up through abstract layering of plaid and military camouflage motifs. Fragments of embroidered olive branch patterns were inspired by Turkish folk costume.

TEMPORAL MEDITATIONS (p. 21) *Spring/Summer 2004*
BETC, Paris, 9 October 2003, 8.30 p.m.
Chalayan's native Cyprus and its history of migration served as central themes for *Temporal Meditations*. Using genetic anthropology as a key in determining ethnic movements across space and time, Chalayan traced historical migration patterns of Greek and Turkish Cypriots. An image of a large-scale aeroplane served as a backdrop to this show, making ever present the possibility of an eventual exodus. Casual workwear in beige canvas was shown with black and white monochrome cotton dresses, shorts and trousers. Feminine ruffled dresses were cut from patterned fabrics. What seemed to be colorful Hawaiian prints were actually pictures of the Cypriot coastline in the 1950s, one of the most turbulent and violent periods in the island's history. Historical battle scenes were portrayed around a hotel swimming pool against the backdrop of palm trees with a nearby aeroplane ready to depart. The garments, Chalayan said, 'can be viewed as an archaeological talisman, which morphs slivers of past and present, ultimately and perhaps paradoxically becoming a frozen fragment of its own archaeological quest.'

ANTHROPOLOGY OF SOLITUDE ♀ (p. 219) *Autumn/Winter 2004*
Le Grand Hôtel, Paris, 5 March 2004, 12.30 p.m.
For *Anthropology of Solitude*, Chalayan was interested in the definition

of the 'self' not only the initial sense of personal identity as formed during childhood but also the 'national self' and the contemporary 'isolated self'. He elaborated: 'In our technologically driven society, speed and communication have become paradigms underwriting our thoughts, actions and how we perceive ourselves. Consequently, this is creating a new anthropology of the isolated and autonomous individual.' Black coats in fake fur were hooded to represent capsules for solitude. Garments with CD pockets emphasized self-containment sealing off the wearer from the outside world. To convey a nationalistic feeling, prints and jacquards depicted Turkish historical images from the creation of the Republic in 1923 up through the 1950s.

PLACE/NON-PLACE 🍸 (p. 214) *Menswear, Autumn/Winter 2003*
Event at Heathrow Airport, London, 4 May 2004
Place/Non-Place was an interactive event coinciding with Chalayan's Autumn/Winter 2003 menswear collection of the same name. Inspired by French anthropologist Marc Augé's description of airports as 'non-places', Chalayan became interested in the idea of temporarily turning a non-place into a 'place' through an event instigated by clothes. Chalayan attached labels inside his garments, inviting buyers to gather at Heathrow about 10 months after the collection was available. After 10 months, one person turned up at Heathrow and met with two members of Chalayan's design team, who took photos and interviewed this individual. Chalayan described his intention: 'Many garments containing pockets for specially collected objects could have been bought along to the event, where strangers could have created a dialogue through the significance of these objects for them or by simply sharing their reasons for buying the clothes etc, ultimately garments becoming a token for communication whilst also turning the non-place into a temporary place.'

BLINDSCAPE 〰️〰️ (p. 156) *Spring/Summer 2005*
Couvent des Cordeliers, Paris, 7 October 2004, 5.30 p.m.
Chalayan has noted that '*Blindscape* was originally inspired by how a seeing person with worldly references can try to attempt to see the world from a blind person's viewpoint.' For the designer, the states of sleeping and dreaming are the only moments when the world of the seeing and the blind overlap. Consequently, Chalayan blindfolded himself and sketched the first part of this collection, designing the basics of a wardrobe in a simplified form. Inspired by sleep, shirts, shorts and light summer dresses were made from cottons in blue and white pinstripes. Symbolizing a nightmare, dramatic prints of sea monsters were used as patterns for the third and final grouping. As the ferocious sea died down, sexy blue beaded 'water dresses' emulated the calm and tranquil water after a stormy dream.

GENOMETRICS 🔺 (p. 250) *Autumn/Winter 2005*
France-Amérique, Paris, 3 March 2005, 6.00 p.m.
The term *genometrics* describes the biometric analyses of chromosomes and stresses the application of statistical methods to the study of genomic data. 'The collection evolved from the idea of how different individuals living in London would fit into London life depending on the reaction of their DNA sequences to the London soundscape through a specifically developed programme,' Chalayan explained. 'Each letter of their DNA sequence was mapped out on the garment and "sensitized" to react to different sounds which make up the soundscape. The shapes seen within the animation were frozen at a peak point in action creating the basis for design.' Tapestry elements, shaved carpet weaves in coated cottons and jumbo corduroys were used to give life to the impressive sculptural shapes taken directly from the sound test experiments. DNA as a theme is also used by Chalayan in his 2005 film *Absence Presence*.

HELIOTROPICS 〰️〰️ (p. 160) *Spring/Summer 2006*
Carrousel du Louvre, Paris, 6 October 2005, 6.00 p.m.
In his work, Chalayan has explored different archetypical women. At first this archetype was modest and discrete, evolving into a more sexual, desirable and empowered figure. In *Heliotropics*, Chalayan presented short, sexy and body-conscious clothes for his new heroine. By concealing or revealing parts of the body, Chalayan created sculptural silhouettes that accentuated the feminine figure. A biological term, heliotropism refers to the growth of plants, particularly flowers, in response to the stimulus of sunlight. Chalayan established the relation between human beings and nature by exploring a cross-section of

aesthetic genres such as art nouveau and rococo that present an ornamental stylization of nature. The dresses in ivory or black and multi-coloured prints trace the female form like beautiful flowers. Reminiscent of blossom stems, piping contours and structures the garments becoming more imposing in the finale dresses to form rope-like elements that delimit boundaries and reference VIP velvet ropes that are used to separate people.

REPOSE 🕯️ (p. 105) *Autumn/Winter 2006*
Carrousel du Louvre, Paris, 1 March 2006, 12 p.m.
Through *Repose*, Chalayan continued to explore the notions of travel and movement. Whereas in his collection *Echoform*, Chalayan presented neck cushions and an *Aeroplane Dress* as a metaphor for speed, with *Repose* he mixed in a domestic reference. Household furniture elements were incorporated into the silhouettes to combine travel with a domestic setting. Wood-grain-printed dévoré silks, exaggerated neck lines – reminiscent of gentlemen's club chairs – patterned seat covers and Victorian upholstery allude to the comfort of the home. The state of the body may be in movement but the accoutrements of a comfortable sedentary life were ingrained in these designs. After the stormy dreams presented in *Blindscape* (Spring/Summer 2005), *Repose* offered a restful pause.

ONE HUNDRED AND ELEVEN ◯ (p. 132) *Spring/Summer 2007*
Palais Omnisport de Bercy, Paris, 4 October 2006, 6.00 p.m.
Chalayan is inspired by the way in which world events, including wars, revolutions, political and social changes have shaped fashion over the course of a century. Through *One Hundred and Eleven*, he commented on time and history in a collaboration with Swarovski that celebrated the crystal company's 111th anniversary. As early as 2001, Chalayan had begun to explore the concept of morphing in his film for the *Mapreading* (Autumn/Winter 2001) collection. With *One Hundred and Eleven*, he pushed the idea further, creating a series of hand-constructed mechanical dresses which, as parts moved, physically morphed from one era's style to another. Representing a fashion history retrospective of over a century, Chalayan began with a high-necked, full-length Victorian silhouette dating from 1895 that metamorphosed, at the touch of a button, to a looser-fitting dress that rose to the calf in a 1910 style before transforming into a distinctive 1920s flapper dress. With six morphing dresses, Chalayan lept through decades and iconic silhouettes engineering a spectacular vision of fashion and its vocabulary. The soundtrack provided a contrast to the stunning technological feats by bringing together audio fragments taken from jet engines, trench warfare and aerial bombings.

AIRBORNE ◯ (p. 144) *Autumn/Winter 2007*
Carreau du Temple, Paris, 28 February 2007, 8.30 p.m.
Presented in four parts: Spring, Summer, Autumn and Winter, *Airborne* commented on how cycles of the weather had parallels with death/life cycles of the body. Chalayan has been constantly interested in the weather as an external power that controls our lives, an inimitable force that is in a constant state of flux. Through the magic of 15,600 LED lamps, combined with crystal displays, the first dress on the catwalk depicted an underwater life form representing summer. High-tech gear was also included, in hats designed to give off a red glow in the dark winter. From protective structures inspired by Japanese samurai armour to fresh blue and white striped dresses paired with shiny rubber leggings, Chalayan explored, in a poetic manner, the resistance to and harmony with nature.

READINGS ▨ (p. 183) *Spring/Summer 2008*
A film by Hussein Chalayan, premiered at Galerie Magda Danysz, Paris, 3 October 2007, 8.00 p.m.
In a film collaboration with Nick Knight's fashion broadcasting company SHOWstudio, Chalayan has once again asserted his commitment to the exploration of technology. Inspired by ancient sun worship and contemporary celebrity status, Chalayan looks at the 'myriad ways different historical, ethnic and religious cultures have worshipped "higher sources" over the centuries'. *Readings* focuses on the cycle of energy between the devotional object and its audience: how icons are made, the rapidity with which they are now accepted into the modern world and how they survive. Hundreds of forms drawn from diverse

cultures were morphed and reduced to two composite silhouettes: 'Greek' and 'Jarab' (Jewish/Arab). These composites offered the key stories of the collection along with two sub-themes: Print, arrived at through layering of printed fabrics, and Pois, named after the spotted chiffon from which its dresses are made. The finale showcases, in Chalayan's words, 'the collection's sun-worshipping origins, mapping out an icon's projected and received energy using lasers.' Decorated with Swarovski crystals, the dresses were fitted with 200 moving lasers that gave off high-intensity red beams creating a spectacular light performance. Music was provided by Antony Hegarty of Antony and the Johnsons.

GRAINS AND STEEL ♟ (p. 221) *Autumn/Winter 2008*
Musée de l'Homme, Paris, 27 February 2008, 8.00 p.m.
In *Grains and Steel*, Chalayan explored the evolution of humanity and its transformation from the Stone Age to the Steel era. A five-person a cappella group set the tone, producing an extraordinary array of abstract and realistic sounds – from outer space, a jungle folkloric and religious vocals. Soft black dresses, asymmetrical, draped and with printed stone patterns hinted at Chalayan's interest in life sciences, where human behaviour and cultural codes are brought together through anthropological stories of space and technology. Like explorers from another age, the two models of the finale came out from the dark dressed in tight black one-piece suits with protruding light elements that were to guide them through the Big Bang of the universe.

INERTIA ♟ (p. 110) *Spring/Summer 2009*
Palais Omnisport de Bercy, Paris, 1 October 2008, 7.30 p.m.
The concept of speed was the focus of this collection. Chalayan noted: 'Speed has become the essence of all facets of how we live our lives today, where daily processes are speeded up to achieve as much as possible in the quickest possible time... The crash represents the result of this fast-paced living and of the ever-growing emergency. The corset reference represents therapy. It is the idea that the pieces (of the body) are held together via these surgical corsets.' Envisioned as three sequences, *Inertia* employed images of 'body cavities' and 'car graves' printed on bonded jersey with foam edging in metallic grey and Porsche red. Organic forms in the silhouettes' construction symbolized the natural world which was overtaken by violent images of broken windscreens, embellished embroideries and rubber edging. 'Finally,' Chalayan added, 'the body became the "event" of a crash where garments caught in the midst of speed simultaneously embodied the cause and effect of a crash in one moment.' With the live smashing of dozens of glasses lined up in a bar inset, the finale brought together five models frozen in motion on a revolving podium wearing spectacular molded latex mini-dresses hand-painted with images of crashed automobiles.

EARTHBOUND ♟ (p. 118) *Autumn/Winter 2009*
Couvent des Cordeliers, Paris, 8 March 2009, 3.00 p.m.
Earthbound was inspired by changing environments, the desire to stay routed amidst a constant state of flux and the way in which even the development of our architectural landscape can be indicative of the body's gradual development. Chalayan used architecture, building processes and building materials to translate the urban London landscape into clothing. He wrote: 'Concrete foundations are evoked through specially developed bonded grey puffa, whilst sculptural fabric in fine black, white and grey weave is worked into organically draped mini-dresses, which suggest concrete in its flowing liquid state. A photographic print of grey asphalt pavement moves the concept from foundations to ground level and adds texture... Finally, bright turquoise and coral embellished prints of scaffolding and stone move into a section of specially created, vibrantly coloured moulded leather busts and bottoms attached to soft concrete-print leather dresses. These elements are incorporated to create the impression of architecture, blurring the gap between reality and fantasy.'

DOLCE FAR NIENTE ✐ (p. 188) *Spring/Summer 2010*
Couvent des Cordeliers, Paris, 4 October 2009, 3.00 p.m.
With the air of a 1950s band leader, Chalayan appeared on stage as the master of ceremonies for his *Dolce Far Niente* collection. Wearing a slicked-back, made-to-measure wig, a pencil moustache and sporting an Yves Saint Laurent dark suit, Chalayan narrated in French a description of each of the six distinct design groups that composed the collection:

1950s silhouette crossed with Mongolian technique, evening dress in a minimalist style with a masculine touch, 1950s viewed through the 1990s, towards the beach, dolce far niente on the way to Deauville, Jacobs Ladder. Progressing through five decades of style, Chalayan gave a modern edge to grown-up glamour. Tailoring with shirting, floor-length dresses in jersey, black leather and white denim, navy blue stripes printed onto organza and white suede were used to create clean, modern and sophisticated silhouettes that sculpted the body. To conjure imagery of the French seaside resort of Deauville, Chalayan used a navy silk plissé with a milk-like fabric to represent ocean waves. In the last section, *Jacobs Ladder*, the garments were punctuated by high-gloss brooches in the form of climbing hands representing, Chalayan said, 'ideas of ascension and aspiration in the present day'.

MIRAGE ⛰ (p. 254) *Autumn/Winter 2010*
Couvent des Cordeliers, Paris, 7 March 2010, 3.00 p.m
With *Mirage*, Chalayan continued to reinterpret the idea of the 'journey' – literal and metaphorical, physical and transcendental. The collection evolved from the concept of an American road trip and how a journey can shape a woman's wardrobe. He noted: 'I am interested in identifying the details that bind a garment to a location and the dialogue between identity and place, which are ongoing themes in my work. The archetypal representation of The American Road Trip appealed to me greatly, as it offered a rich source of inspiration to drive the exploration of this theme further.' Across a diverse array of states and terrains, from city to sea, through mountains and over deserts, the journey begins in New York then looks to the Pennsylvania Amish community for inspiration. The glamour of Texan beauty pageants was present in elements such as sashes twisted and trapped between layers of encrusted lace and chiffon, draped as if they had encountered a hurricane, which are common in the area. The proximity of Texas to the Mexican border was hinted at through use of bright wools in red, lilac and yellow that had been knitted to form ruffles, or intricately crocheted. A leather hat and caplet combination connote the exploration of the great expanses of Utah. Arriving in Hollywood, Chalayan evoked 'the elegance of Silver Screen starlets with floor-length black crepe dresses split to the thigh and invaded with pleated inserts that become a conceptual interpretation of the red-carpet gown.'

SAKOKU ♟ (p. 226) *Spring/Summer 2011*
A film by Hussein Chalayan, premiered at Galerie Deborah Zafman, Paris, 1 to 7 October 2010
For this collection, Chalayan did not present a fashion show but instead produced a film, which he directed. Entitled *Sakoku* or 'locked country', the title is the name of Japan's foreign relations policy of isolation, which, until the mid-19th century, banned almost all foreigners from entering the country and any Japanese from leaving under penalty of death. Chalayan explored how shadow, water, architecture, technology, theatre, costume, poetry and isolation all affect Japanese culture. He said: 'Japan is saturated with disembodied experiences in a decentreed space where event is born out of the choreography of ceremony and the simulation of thought.' In six themes, Chalayan presented an abstract take on Japan: *decentred, wrapping in transition, shadow reading, imminence of water, haiku* and *floating body*. Chalayan used wide panels of *broderie anglaise* to enclose the body like a gift waiting to be opened. Mesh fabrics recalled the wicker sliding doors used to divide Japanese interior spaces. Jade green, fuchsia pink, earthy olive, mustard and light beige are applied in blocks following the colour tradition of kabuki.

ACKNOWLEDGEMENTS

By the time this book reaches the shelves, it will have been nearly four years since we first met Charles Miers from Rizzoli. Working on this book has become a daily routine for me and my team, and, writing this, it already feels peculiar that the work is about to end. Firstly, I would sincerely like to thank Charles Miers for believing in my work and for giving me this amazing opportunity to share the processes and personal sketches for all my collections and other projects, which have been an inseparable part of my life for the last 16 years. Also at Rizzoli, I would also like to thank Ellen Nidy and Maria Pia Gramaglia, and copyeditor Amoreen Armetta, for all the work and cooperative energy they put into making this book happen.

When we never have to explain our thoughts to others because we feel they already know or understand, we become complacent communicators. In scenarios where you have to articulate yourself to others in order that they 'really' understand, you can create clarity for yourself and improve the way you think and communicate. This is exactly what has happened to me in the journey of this book. Through focusing on the connections between all the work done throughout the years, I feel I now have more clarity about the best language needed to explain the thought and design processes also for the future.

The tour guide on this journey, Robert Violette, has undoubtedly been the key hero bringing all the elements together beautifully in this book. Robert, despite being a successful publisher himself (Violette Editions), not only so humbly accepted to be the editor of this book, he has done it with such remarkable dedication like it was his own baby.

I would also like to thank Studio Frith, one of the most refined graphic design studios around. Frith Kerr and Amy Preston have achieved the most thoughtful graphic realization I could have hoped for. Thanks also to the support staff at Violette Editions, especially Naomi Macintosh for the painstaking work needed to document and sort all my drawings, and to assistant editor Tamsin Perrett, retoucher Steve Evans and proofreader Kate Crockett.

Grateful thanks to the authors of the texts in this book: to Emily King, who pressed very interesting buttons in my brain whilst looking at the work from a broader cultural perspective; to Sarah Mower, with whom I nearly cried and laughed about the past in the midst of making connections with my approach to design; to Susannah Frankel, for the highly sensitive and enlightening observations of my processes and the past and present of my work; to Rebecca Lowthorpe, for highlighting our Central Saint Martins roots, and how unexpectedly life can turn out for a fashion student she had as a close friend; to Pamela Golbin, for the painstaking effort she put into gathering and presenting my ideas for every single collection, all with great eloquence; and, finally, to Judith Clark, to whom I owe the power with which each chapter of this book is communicated, whose associations and connections of my work to so many other rich facets of life will almost become new briefs in themselves.

Without the patience and the belief of Milly Patrzalek, my long-time operations manager, and Claudia Bothe, one of our new shining members, it would have been impossible to gather information needed to complete this project, I thank them both immensely.

I would like also to thank specially those whom I think of as family members: Alex de Betak and his team, Barbara Fourneau, John Pfeiffer, Paco Raynal, Violaine Etienne, Benedicte Fournier and Olivier Jégu, for the staging and the choreography of my shows since 1998. This is a truly valuable relationship for me and one of the most enjoyable collaborations in the whole process. Alex is the person I speak to about every collection and what I am trying to convey in a presentation. Without you, Alex, the hardship of showing collections would not have been rewarded and honoured the way they have been. Endless gratitude.

Special thanks to Björk Guðmundsdóttir for her early and continued support of my work.

I would like to express my gratitude to Nadja Swarovski and her team, which has included Pascale Montaner and Anna Chapman. Without Nadja's enthusiasm we would have never been able to realize many of the projects that have impacted the Chalayan house in such a powerful way. I would like to thank Han Nefkens for making many installations possible, and José Teunissen for being the best mediator and curator of all these pieces done for Han.

To Yuko Hasegawa and Susie Allen for their endless belief.

Thank you, Marie-Claude Beaud, for making so much special work happen whilst at MUDAM Luxembourg. And thank you to Béatrice Salmon at the Musée des Arts Décoratifs for inviting us to show years of work at the museum – it is more than an honour.

I would like to thank ultra-specially Chris Moore, Maxine and all at Catwalking for show images that make up a majority of this book; we would have been lost without your help.

Big thanks to Marcus Tomlinson and Nick Knight for providing so much special imagery of my work over the years. For their permission to include magnificent editorial photography, I would also like to thank: Richard Avedon, Mark Borthwick, Donald Christie, Sofia Coppola, Horst Diekgerdes, Warren du Preez and Nick Thornton Jones, Nathaniel Goldberg, Friedmann Hauss, Nick Knight, Peter Lindbergh, Alexi Lubomirski, Mert Alas and Marcus Piggott, Jochen Manz, Raymond Meier, Tom Munro, Barnaby Roper and Scott Lyon, Michael Sanders, Stephane Sednaoui, Sølve Sundsbø, Mario Testino, Inez van Lamsweerde and Vinoodh Matadin, Paul Wetherell, Troy Word. Gratitude also to the Richard Avedon Foundation for allowing us the use of the cover image.

I would like to offer special thanks to: Christopher Laszlo and Milly Patrzalek, who, like family members, have spent the longest time ever in my company supporting the journey along the way, as well as Lena Wells for sticking with us and leading my Puma team; Izumi Harada for her hearty dedication, Elizabeth Burns, Dragana Rikanovic, Riyo Yokoi, Petra Carstensen, Davina Ebikeme, Pavlina Dedicova, Helen Cooper, Maki Ichikawa, Jane How, Pinky Ghundale, Daria Sokolova, Jodie Barnes, Sarah Zigrand, Stuart Roberts, Anne Babel, Lucyna Plocek, Beverley Eaton, Cass Dicker, Medea Moons, Claudia Bothe, Adam Wright, Joe Scott, Paul Topen, Maija Komulainen, Murat Pilevneli, Andree Cooke, Emma Greenhill, Suzy Menkes, Susanne Tide Frater, Caroline Roux, Sonia Eram, Sally Singer, Giorgio Belloli, Karla Otto, Thibault Rivrain, Seda Lafci, Fusun and Faruk Eczacibasi, Esra Ekmekci, Greg Hilty, Jaymin and Janjri Triverdi, Stephen Brackman, Sunil Chopra, Philip Stinson, Mr Okuda, Mr Ogura, Hiromi Ushigome, Akiko Hamazaki-Rastoul, Rob Edkins, Noel Stewart, Scott Wilson, Jean-Paul Dessy, Eugene Souleiman, Franco Pene, Valeria Bargiacchi, Giulliano Marcheschi, Pat McGrath, Jefferson Hack, Bettina Oldenburg, Tilda Swinton, Ivan Patcev, Tricia and Terry Jones,

Alex de Betak, *Afterwords*, Autumn/Winter 2000.

Zoe Smith, Jessica Lomax, Tim Lee, Ebru Ercon, Paolo Gabrielli, Stuart Adams, Tristan Gilby, Berndt Keller, Sylvia Perico, Hugh Devlin, David Leary, William Moen, Chris Levine, Rachel Alsbury, Darryl Matthews, Cedric Edon, Alice Goldie, Andrea Rado Hinks, Adele Clarke, Muriel Poncet, Bennu Gerede, Deyan Sudjic, Donna Loveday, Ria Hawthorn and all at the Design Museum, Sue Ann Van der Jipp, Mark Wilson and all at the Groninger Museum, Caroline Burstein and Mrs Burstein at Browns.

I would like to thank Jochen Zeitz, for giving me the opportunity to become the design director at Puma, and Melody Jensbach-Harris at Puma, for her continued support.

On a personal note I would like to thank these family members: My heroine mother, Sevil Ozel; my dad, Ata Chalayan; Melih Yoru (for the golden support), Sevim Erdal, Tomur Akpinar, Tayfun Erdal, Ozen Mevsimler, Fetanet Sonuc Can, Lebibe Sonuc Veysi, Ozlem Ozel, Zehra Balman, Misli Alan, Mehmet Ozel; my grandparents, Hussein and Fetanet Chalayan; my grandfather, Ali Riza Ozel, and my guardian-angel grandmother, Zehra Ozel.

Thank you to all my friends – you know who you are.

Hussein Chalayan

FILM CREDITS

AEROPLANE DRESS (not illustrated) *1999*
Directed by: Marcus Tomlinson
Produced by: Premiere Heure
Director of photography: Matthieu Vadepied
Executive producer: Elisabeth Fabri

AFTERWORDS (not illustrated) *2000*
Directed by: Marcus Tomlinson
Produced by: Caspar Delaney at 400 Films
Director of photography: Stephan Blackman
Edited by: Rick Lawley and Lisa Gunning at The Whitehouse

PLACE TO PASSAGE ☕ (p.104) *2003*
Written and directed by: Hussein Chalayan
Featuring: Bennu Gerede
Producer: Susie Allen
Tribe Art Director: Jo Maundrell
Music by: Jean-Paul Dessy
Post Production: Neutral (3D Animation, Special Effects, Editing and Soundscape)

TEMPORAL MEDITATIONS (not illustrated) *2003*
Written and directed by: Hussein Chalayan
Featuring: Mark Segal, Sophia Hill (child), Yannis Spanos
Executive producer: Debbie Stylianidis
Director of photography: Christos Karamanis
Edited by: Fani Ziozia
Music by: Mercan Dede, Jean-Paul Dessy, Band of Susans, Kudsi Erguner
Sponsors: Pitti Immagine (Florence, Italy) and Kino TV and Movie Productions (Athens, Greece)

ANAESTHETICS (p.14) *2004*
Written and directed by: Hussein Chalayan
Featuring: Bennu Gerede *and* Eda Akman, Umut Çaglar, Junichi Hıraga, Alican Yücesoy, Minure Damla Dogar, Ender Tahran, Göksel Aktas
Produced by: Production Team of Turkey (PTT), Istanbul
Executive producers: Tunay Vural & Asu Sipsak
Director of photography: Gökhan Atilmıis
Edited by: Aylin Zoi Tinel
Music by: Jean-Paul Dessy
Set production and supervision: Dream Design Factory (DDF), Istanbul

ABSENT PRESENCE ⌐ (p.86) *2005*
Written and directed by: Hussein Chalayan
Featuring: Tilda Swinton
Curated by: Beral Madra
Project producer: Murat Pilevneli
Film producer: Pinky Ghundale
Director of photography: Alessandra Scherillo
Edited by: Elise Traversi
Visual effects: Ethic Productions
Sponsors: Turquality, Garanti Bank, Garanti Shop and Miles, Republic of Turkey, Ministry of Foreign Affairs
This project was specially produced for the Turkish Pavillion at the 51st Venice Biennale
Sponsors: 21st-Century Museum of Contemporary Art, Kanazawa; Musée d'art Moderne Grand Duke Jean (MUDAM), Luxembourg; Anima, Istanbul; and Mr. Ömer Koç

COMPASSION FATIGUE) 🝔 (p.165) *2006*
Written and directed by: Hussein Chalayan
Cast: Sema Simsek, Ahu Yagtu, Selma Ergeç, Özge Ulusoy
Produced by: Karma Productions
Executive producer: Yavuz Öztop
Director of photography: Askin Sagiroglu
Sponsor: Garanti Gallery

I AM SAD LEYLA (ÜZGÜNÜM LEYLA) 🝔 (p.166) *2010*
Directed by: Hussein Chalayan
Performed by: Sertab Erener
Curated by: Greg Hilty
Executive producer: Pinky Ghundale
Vav Film Group: Sila Bektas Sayın
Edited by: Aylin Zoi Tinel
Music by: Tarık Sezer